FAIRY TALE
Sewing

20 Whimsical Toys, Dolls and Softies

HEIDI BOYD

Fons&Porter

CINCINNATI, OH

Contents

Introduction

ONE OF THE JOYS OF BEING A TEACHER, grandparent or parent is reading stories out loud to our children. We travel to wondrous places in our imaginations and share the adventures of heroines and heroes. Whether it's quiet time, sitting by the fire or snuggling under the covers at bedtime, by sharing beautifully written and illustrated stories, we ignite a love of reading while passing timeless legends to the next generation.

Classic fairy tales are an integral part of our storytelling culture; most tales were shared verbally long before they landed in print in the early 1800s. While some of the original Hans Christian Andersen and The Brothers Grimm stories can be dark, many of the retold versions are wonderfully empowering. Lisa Campbell Ernst authored two such books: in her *The Gingerbread Girl*, a feisty cookie outsmarts the fox by lassoing him with a licorice rope, and a capable tractor-driving Grandma takes care of the pesky fox in *Little Red Riding Hood, A Newfangled Prairie Tale*.

Creating original toys based on beloved old tales and spunky new ones reinforces the importance of reading. The predictability of a well-known character like the Princess and the Pea or Puss in Boots will comfort your child; they're the superheroes of the book world. By placing the actual character in their hands, you're inspiring them to rescript the stories and act out their own adventures. All the projects in this book can be props for open-ended pretend play. The gorgeous fabric vegetables in the Stone Soup Pot might turn up in your next "restaurant" meal. The pop-up Castle can set the stage for countless dragon battles or tea parties. The familiar pig and dwarf characters in the play totes can move beyond their classic tales, teaming together to explore the exciting world of your home. And who says the Little Mermaid has to put up with the evil sea witch's curse? She can live happily in the human world and swim through a sea of blankets at night.

Designing this book was an absolute joy; you couldn't find a more inspiring cast of human, animal and magical characters. I strove to simplify construction so that every project is easy and fun to stitch, while ensuring the finished creation would appeal to a discerning young audience. Enjoy perusing the photo gallery of projects. Once you reach the instructions, you'll find of most of the designs require a yard or less of fabric. Dig right into your fabric stash and see what you already have on hand; within an hour or two you could be stitching eyes onto a finished toy. It's impossible to suppress a smile when you're stuffing a fluffy dragon, snipping apart a unicorn's mane, stitching up troll pants or attaching little pig tails. By sewing for a child in your life, you'll reawaken your own inner child. Best of all, by creating a handmade keepsake, you'll become your child's creative hero/heroine.

Happy Stitching!
Heidi

Who's that tramping over my bridge?
—*THREE BILLY GOATS GRUFF*, NORWEGIAN FAIRY TALE

Troll
See instructions on page 27.

Puss in Boots
See instructions on page 31.

I would gladly give all the hundreds of years that I have to live to be a human being only for one day, and to have the hope of knowing the happiness of that glorious world above the stars.
—*THE LITTLE MERMAID*, HANS CHRISTIAN ANDERSEN

The Little Mermaid
See instructions on page 36.

Grandmother! What big eyes you have!
—*LITTLE RED RIDING HOOD*, CHARLES PERRAULT

Little Red Riding Hood and the Wolf
(reversible)
See instructions on page 40.

7

> *Even now, between the breaking waves, you may sometimes hear the warm breathing of the Unicorns close by.*
> —*UNICORNS! UNICORNS!*, GERALDINE MCCAUGHREAN

Unicorn
See instructions on page 44.

Shoemaker's Elves
See instructions on page 47.

9

Very well then, I will do it myself.
—*THE LITTLE RED HEN,* RUSSIAN FOLKTALE

Little Red Hen Embroidery
See instructions on page 56.

*"I'm not an ugly duckling,"he honked.
"I'm a beautiful swan!"*
—*THE UGLY DUCKLING,*
HANS CHRISTIAN ANDERSEN

Ugly Duckling Embroidery
See instructions on page 51.

*But as he fell, he ceased to be a frog, and
became all at once a prince.*
—*THE FROG PRINCE,* THE BROTHERS GRIMM

Frog Prince Embroidery
See instructions on page 54.

*Cinderella sat down, and, putting
the slipper to her foot, he found that
it went on very easily.*
—*CINDERELLA*, CHARLES PERRAULT

Cinderella's Shoes
See instructions on page 58.

None of my books ever told me that dragons purred!
—*THE RELUCTANT DRAGON,*
KENNETH GRAHAME

Dragon
See instructions on page 62.

The king ordered the castle's great brass gates to be opened so that the tidings of peace and joy might spread through all the land.

—*SAINT GEORGE AND THE DRAGON, MARGARET HODGES*

Medieval Castle
See instructions on page 65.

*Stone Soup Pot and Veggies
See instructions on page 68.*

14

These are magical beans, Jack. Plant them at night and by morning they will grow right up to the sky.

—*JACK AND THE BEANSTALK*, ENGLISH FAIRY TALE

*Jack and the Beanstalk Pillow
See instructions on page 76.*

*Rapunzel Pillow,
See instructions on page 73.*

Rapunzel, Rapunzel, let down your hair!

—*RAPUNZEL*, THE BROTHERS GRIMM

Aladdin's Lamp
See instructions on page 79.

"Little pig, little pig, let me come in."
"No, not by the hair on my chinny chin chin!"
—*THE THREE LITTLE PIGS*, ENGLISH FAIRY TALE

Cottage Tote with Doll Sets
See instructions on page 83.

Mirror, mirror, on the wall, who is the fairest of them all?
—*SNOW WHITE AND THE SEVEN DWARFS*, FAIRY TALE

Thumbelina
See instructions on page 90.

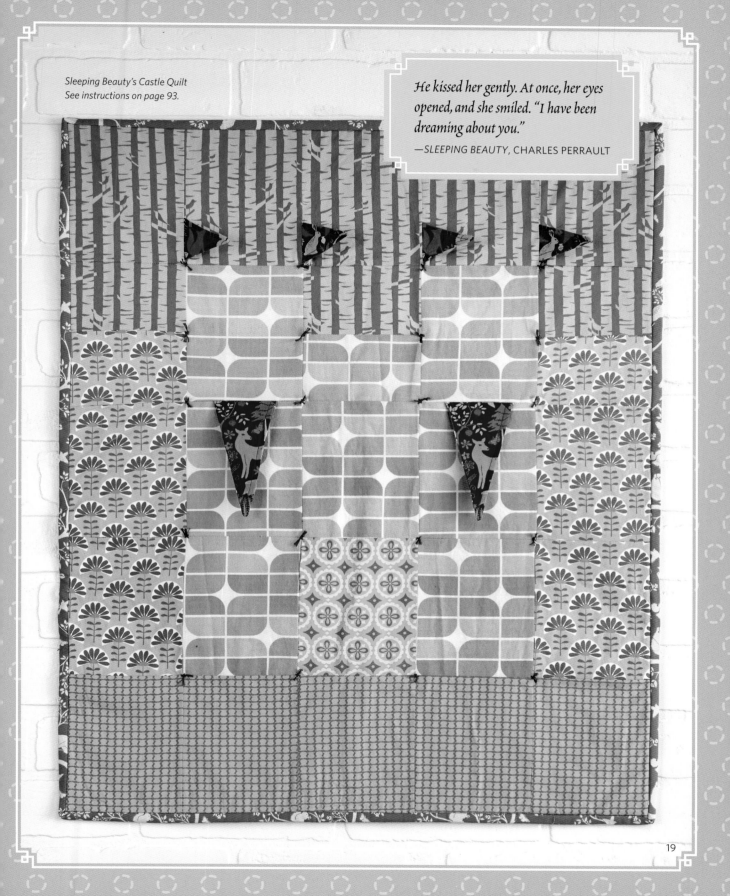

Sleeping Beauty's Castle Quilt
See instructions on page 93.

He kissed her gently. At once, her eyes opened, and she smiled. "I have been dreaming about you."

—*SLEEPING BEAUTY*, CHARLES PERRAULT

The Princess and the Pea Playset
See instructions on page 98.

Materials, Tools & Techniques

CREATING TOYS AND SOFTIES IS MUCH EASIER THAN YOU MIGHT EXPECT. The best part is that your efforts are always rewarded with hugs and smiles. You may already have all the fabric you need to make most of the projects in this book, but don't let me stop you from seeking out the perfect new cotton collection. A quick run to your local fabric shop will take care of the rest of the items on the materials lists.

BASIC MATERIALS

Printed Cotton Fabric

I don't want to admit how much time I spend selecting fabric. Like a kid in a candy store, I have trouble focusing in the sea of color and pattern. I have commandeered large sections of my favorite local quilt shop arranging different patterns together. If you don't have the luxury of a shop close by and you're buying fabric online, stick to a single fabric collection for a project. It's difficult to match colors from different collections without seeing the true colors in person. If you have some of the fabrics for a project but not all, slip them in a clear bag and bring them shopping with you to make sure the colors will all work together. Time spent choosing the perfect fabric can't be underestimated.

Felt

No-fray and easy-to-stitch felt is widely used for faces, embellishments and hair. Its weight adds structure to many of the designs in this book, especially the Stone Soup Pot. There's no substitute for good-quality felt; look for at least 20% wool content. Bamboo felt is a great "green" alternative, but stay away from acrylic felts that pull apart and pill. I use National Nonwovens Woolfelt and am fortunate to have a great color stash. You can purchase small sheets or single yards (meters) of felt to build a color selection; start with a skin tone, a choice of hair colors, tan, black, red, purple, pink, blue and green.

Polyester Blend Fabrics

Kids respond to variety and texture; don't limit yourself to the quilt fabric aisles. Rich sequined brocade and silk polyester bring sparkle to Aladdin's Lamp. Smooth and soft polyester adds warmth and softness to the Dragon, Unicorn and Jack and Rapunzel's pillows. Fleece is the easiest polyester to stitch; like felt, it doesn't fray and shares its sturdy structure. The Troll showcases fleece's versatility and cuddle-bility. It's important not to substitute the specified polyester blends with cotton, as their stretch is what makes the design work. Flex your creative muscles and let the projects inspire you to branch into new fabrics.

Interfacing

Hidden inside many creations is a vital structural layer. The Mermaid and Princess linen dolls use fusible fleece to stabilize the fabric stretch while adding strength to withstand the embroidered stitches. Fusible fleece also adds weight and structure to the Princess and the Pea bedding. Pellon Craft-Fuse, an iron-on fabric backing, adds structure but not bulk to Aladdin's Lamp. Be sure to follow the manufacturer's instructions for any interfacing you use.

Polyester Stuffing and Batting

Almost all the creations in this book require stuffing. I always have bags of polyester stuffing (or fiberfill) at the ready; it doesn't lump and easily squeezes into tiny places. For the Princess and the Pea mattresses, I switched to cut rectangles of rolled polyester batting to help retain the square shape. I use a more expensive, high-quality natural wool batting for the Castle Quilt, but you could easily substitute what you have on hand, including a couple of yards (meters) of fleece.

Hook-and-Loop Fastener

The ideal closure for children's projects, hook-and-loop fastener doesn't pose the inherent choking hazard or difficulty that buttons do, and it comes in a variety of colors. Hook-and-loop fastener is integral to the structure and functionality of the Medieval Castle and the play totes.

Elastic

A few projects in this book require a little stretch. I used small lengths of elastic to fasten Little Red Riding Hood's cape and to curl the Troll's tail. Elastic can be purchased by the package or by the yard (meter).

Bias Tape, Rickrack, Ribbon, Cording and Pompom Trim

Don't scrimp on the finishing touches! Collect an assortment in varying widths; tiny rickrack and ¼" (6mm) bias tape are my favorites. Most of these projects use small lengths of trim, perfect for using up scraps that you already have on hand. Trims aren't just an embellishment; they finish the cut fabric edges and prevent fraying on Cinderella's shoes and Little Red Riding Hood's cape.

Floss

All of the doll and animal faces in this book are stitched with embroidery floss. I'm partial to DMC and keep a stash of colors at the ready. Grab a basic selection of colors to get started; for these projects you'll need red, pink, orange, yellow, mustard, gold, green, bright-green, light-blue, blue, brown, black and white. Floss can easily get knotted up; wrap unused lengths around a scrap of cardboard, and store them in a clear bin.

Sewing Thread

It's a great idea to have a selection of good-quality sewing thread in a variety of colors on hand. I like to pick up assorted boxes when they go on sale. I purchase large spools of off-white quilter's-weight cotton; they last forever and do a great job of sewing through layers of felt and cotton.

Speciality Items

A few of the projects call for specific materials. For example, plastic pellets give the Unicorn's hooves weight and stability, allowing him to stand. Puss in Boots sports a belt buckle. Yarn, felt balls and safety eyes also are also used in these projects. Read through the materials list for your selected project before you a begin to make sure you have everything you need.

BASIC TOOLS

Rotary Cutter, Ruler and Cutting Mat

Cutting straight lines is a challenge without a rotary cutter, clear ruler and cutting mat. I can only imagine what a disaster I'd be without these tools. Remember to change the blade on your rotary cutter often and always close the blade whenever the cutter is not in use.

Scissors

It's essential to dedicate scissors for fabric-only use. Tag them, educate your family, do what you need to do to ensure that your blades will not be dulled by paper. You'll need both a large and small pair: use the large pair for cutting large fabric pieces, and the small pair for cutting smaller pieces and trimming thread ends.

Stuffing Stick, Knitting Needle or Pencil

It's handy to have a tool to help you feed stuffing into tight spots like doll hands and feet, and also to help you turn small sewn pieces right-side out. Sometimes you'll find a wooden stuffing stick packed with your bag of stuffing. If you haven't been gifted one, you can use a knitting needle, chopstick or the eraser end of a pencil.

Sewing machine

A well-running, basic sewing machine is a must. Spare yourself the frustration of being hampered by a machine that isn't working well and take it to a repair shop for a tune-up. You will be rewarded by hours of pleasurable sewing. You won't need any fancy computerized features for the projects in this book. A walking foot would be helpful for stitching through the thick layers of the Castle Quilt.

Hand-Sewing Needles

It's a good idea to have a variety of hand-sewing and embroidery needles. Thicker fabric requires a thicker needle, thinner fabric, a thinner needle.

BASIC TECHNIQUES

Prewash or Not?

Back in the day we were always told to prewash fabrics. That theory has since been tossed out, and now we can enjoy sewing brand-new fabric guilt free. The manufacturing sizing helps to stabilize the fabric. Just don't mix prewashed fabrics with unwashed fabrics, as you want them to shrink evenly in the machine. Felt can never be machine washed, which means many of the projects in the book can only be surface cleaned with a damp cloth.

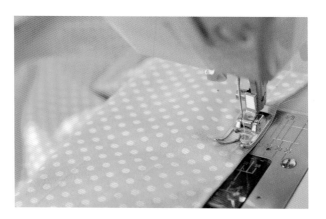

Topstitching

Topstitching is a decorative finishing seam that ensures that the seamed edge lies flat. After you've turned the piece right-side out and pressed it flat, stitch around the edge a second time ¼" (6mm) from the seamed edge. Use the edge of the presser foot to guide the fabric and ensure a seam that is consistently the same distance from the seamed edge.

Pressing

You may not believe it but the iron is really your friend. Don't wrestle with wrinkly fabric; press it flat before you pin it. It's also a worthwhile step to press your seams after stitching, especially before topstitching. Be sure to adjust the iron temperature for synthetic fabrics. Follow package directions when fusing interfacing to your fabric.

Pinning

Pins are essential to hold fabric layers together and prevent shifting. Push the pin down through both layers and then back up to the top ½" (1.3cm) from where you inserted it. Always keep a pincushion close at hand. You won't be popular if family members step on a stray pin.

Right Sides Together

Almost all the instructions begin by asking you to place right sides together. There isn't a wrong side to felt, so don't worry which side faces in. It's easy to find the right side with all the other fabrics. This step ensures that your seams will be hidden on the wrong side (inside) of your creation, after you turn the piece right-side out.

Sewing Seams

Reinforce the beginning and end of each seam by backstitching. Use the edge of your presser foot or the markings on your base plate to guide your fabric; this will ensure a seam that is consistently the same distance from the fabric edge. Stop and remove the straight pins as you stitch.

Trimming Away Excess Fabric

To limit unnecessary bulk, cut away selvedges, especially at corners, before turning your sewing right-side out. First peek on the right side to check your seam, then return to the back side and clip away ⅛" (3mm) of the selvedge edge. Be careful not to unintentionally cut into the seam. Because felt and fleece don't fray, you can trim the curved selvedge close to the seam. Clipping curves, as you would for many garment fabrics, could weaken the selvedge and affect the form of stuffed items.

Stuffing

Use a stuffing stick, knitting needle, chopstick or the eraser end of a pencil to push bits of stuffing into the small areas first and then fill the rest of the creation. Be sure the form is completely filled out as hugging will result in some flattening. Don't go too far the other way; overstuffing will distort the shape.

Hand Sewing Openings Closed

Tuck in the open fabric edges, then pin them together. Use a sewing needle and matching color thread and begin hand stitching the tucked-in fabric sides together. The goal is to blend the new seam with the machine seam. Make small stitches back and forth from one fabric edge to the other, closing the opening.

Preparing the Patterns

All the patterns you need to create these projects are included in the back of the book. Locate the pieces for your project and enlarge to the specified size on a photocopier. Some of the projects are quite large and have large pattern pieces. These pieces will not fit on an 8½" × 11" (21.6cm × 27.9cm) sheet of paper. Print these large pieces out in sections and tape them together to create the full-size pattern.

If you have access to the Internet, you can download the full-size patterns as pdfs. Print them out, then piece them together as indicated. Visit www.sewdaily.com/FairyTaleSewing to download the patterns.

Seam Allowance

Unless otherwise indicated, all projects are sewn with a ¼" (6mm) seam allowance. You may need to add a seam allowance when cutting out your pattern piece. Other projects already include the seam allowance in the pattern piece, and others still require no seam allowance. Always read through your project completely before you start cutting and sewing.

NOTE

Please note that many of these projects contain small pieces that may pose a choking hazard and not be suitable for young children. Please supervise your child during play.

Embroidery Stitch Guide

NOT SURE HOW TO MAKE A STITCH? This guide will show you the basics you need to know. Have no fear, you can always redo a stitch: Simply pull the needle off of the floss and use the needle tip to pull up the floss. Start with your most recent step and pull out all the strands of floss. Continue working your way backwards to your starting point. Rethread the needle and try again; you'll get it right the second time.

Straight Stitch

This is the most common and easiest stitch of all. Simply bring your needle up from behind your work and bring it back down the desired distance from where it emerged.

V-Stitches

V-shaped stitches are formed by making two straight, slanted, connected stitches. The stitches can form a standard V or an inverted V. The appearance of this stitch varies greatly depending on the length or angle of the straight stitches.

Note: The length listed in the project instructions refers to the length of each individual straight stitch making up the V.

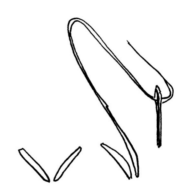

Cross-Stitch

Bring the needle tip up through the bottom right corner of your first cross-stitch. Make a ¼" (6mm) diagonal stitch to the top left corner of the cross-stitch. You've completed half of your first cross-stitch. Continue making the required number of half stitches until you reach the end of the line. Beginning at the bottom left corner of the last stitch made, make a ¼" (6mm) diagonal stitch that intersects the first stitch and ends at the top right corner. Working your way back across the line, complete the remaining half stitches.

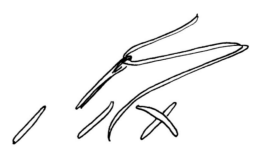

French Knot

Bring the needle up from the back of your work, then pull up the length of your thread. Pierce the needle through a section of fabric alongside the first hole. Wrap the thread three times around the needle tip.

Gently draw the needle up through the loops using your fingers to slide the loops down against the fabric. Bring the needle back down alongside the stack of loops.

Blanket Stitch

Bring the needle up ¼" (6mm) from the fabric edge. Before pulling the needle all the way out, wrap the thread around the needle tip. Start each new stitch a ¼" (6mm) from the last stitch. When encircling a piece of fabric, link the final stitch to the first stitch.

Lazy Daisy Stitch

Bring the needle up at the base of the stitch. Then bring the needle back down right alongside where it emerged. Don't pull all the floss; leave a generous loop that will form the petal.

Bring the needle back up through the top of the petal, inside the floss loop. Make a small vertical straight stitch, trapping the floss loop and holding it in place. Watch your tension; pull this last stitch too tight and you'll flatten the petal.

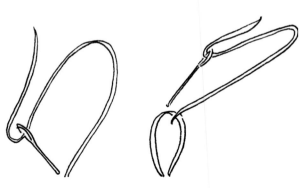

Running Stitch

A running stitch is a connected series of straight stitches in and out, up and down. It can be used both decoratively or functionally.

Troll

EVERY STORY HAS A BAD GUY, and this fuzzy fellow is up for the role. He can guard wooden bridges or pillow forts from unauthorized trespassers. Soft and cuddly, he just might be the cutest curmudgeon around. Easy-to-stitch fleece instantly adds substance to his body, limbs and features.

Note: Add a ¼" (6mm) seam allowance to the indicated pattern pieces.

Dimensions: 12" × 21" (30.5cm × 53.3cm)

MATERIALS

Templates on page 104

1 yard (0.9m) beige fleece

¼ yard (0.2m) brown fleece

½ yard (0.5m) printed cotton

⅛ yard (0.1m) coordinating printed cotton

Scrap of white wool felt

2 black safety eyes

8" (20.3cm) of ½" (1.3cm) elastic

Sewing thread in coordinating colors

Embroidery floss in black

Fur trim, for eyebrows

Fiberfill stuffing

TOOLS

Sewing machine

Scissors

Embroidery and sewing needles

Straight pins

Iron and ironing board

Stuffing stick

1. Using the templates, cut the following pattern pieces adding a ¼" (6mm) seam allowance:
- From the beige fleece, cut 1 body front, 2 body backs, 4 arms, 2 noses, 1 set of ears and 1 set of feet. For the tail, cut a 8¼" × 2½" (21cm × 6.4cm) strip.
- From the brown fleece, cut 1 set of ears and 1 set of feet. Cut three 1" × 2¾" (2.5cm × 7cm) hair strips and one 1½" × 36" (3.8cm × 91.4cm) belt strip.
- From the printed cotton, cut 2 pant fronts, 2 pant backs and 1 base piece.
- From the coordinating cotton fabric, cut five 1¼" × 4" (3.2cm × 10.2cm) belt loops.
- From the white felt, cut 2 teeth.
- From the fur trim, cut two 1" × 2" (2.5cm × 5.1cm) strips for the eyebrows.

2. Placing right sides together, pin 2 sets of arms together. Stitch around the outside edge, leaving the shoulder ends unsewn.

Cut an X in the center of a nose piece. Pin the 2 nose pieces together and stitch around the outside edge.

Placing right sides together, pin a brown foot to each beige foot, making sure you have a left and a right foot with beige on top. Stitch around the outside edge leaving the flat end unsewn.

3. Check all your seams, trim away any excess fabric and turn all pieces right-side out. Feed stuffing into the X cut in the nose and the open ends of the arms and feet. Fill all the appendages; be careful not to overstuff and distort the pieces (Figure 1).

4. Placing right sides together, pin a brown ear piece to each beige ear piece, making sure you create a right ear and a left ear with a beige front. Stitch around the curved outside edge, leaving the straight connecting edge unsewn. Turn the ears right-side out, smooth them flat and topstitch the curved seamed outer ear. Pinch the open center of each ear and sew a 1" (2.5cm) dart from the open end to the curved outer edge (Figure 2). This will narrow the connection portion and create a rounded appendage.

5. Placing right sides together, pin then stitch the pant fronts together along the inside edge. Working on the wrong side, open the connected pant fronts into a single layer and press the seam flat.

Fold down ¼" (6mm) of the top pant edge and press the fold flat. Lay the body front right-side up on your work surface. Lay the pant front, right-side up, over the body. Line up the bottom edges and pin the folded top edge to the troll's tummy.

Make a single seam across the top of the pants, ¼" (6mm) down from the folded edge, sewing through all layers. Make 2 vertical seams down either side of the center pant seam, again sewing through all layers; these seams will attach the middle of the pants to the bottom half of the body piece (Figure 3).

6. Position the stuffed nose, X-cut down, on the body front (Figure 4). Hand-stitch the nose in place with small invisible stitches.

Clip 2 small holes 1" (2.5cm) above either side of the nose for the eyes. Push the screw end of each safety eye into a hole. Working on the wrong side of the body front, slide a plastic backing piece on each screw end until it rests snugly against the fleece. On the right side, hand-stitch a furry eyebrow over each eye (Figure 4).

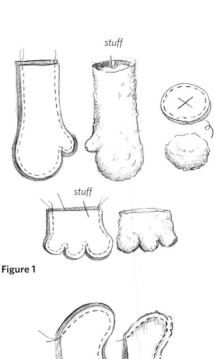

Figure 1

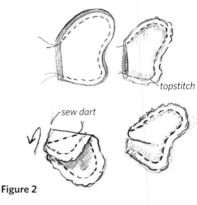

Figure 2

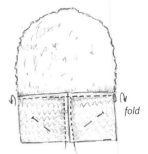

Figure 3   vertical seams

Figure 4

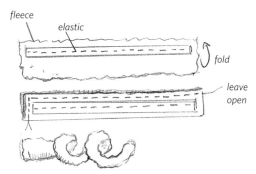

fleece
elastic
fold
leave
open

Figure 5

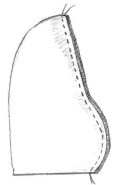

wrong side
tail

Figure 6

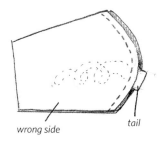

Figure 7

topstitch

Figure 8

7. Using an embroidery needle and black floss, stitch a wide smile under the nose with 10 connected ½" (1.3cm) stitches.

Stack the 2 tooth pieces together and stitch around the outside edge. Leave the flat side open. Turn the tooth right-side out and hand-stitch the opening closed. Leave the thread hanging and use it to sew the flat edge of the tooth to the smile (Figure 4).

Fold each of the 3 hair strips in half lengthwise, wrong sides together, and pin. Machine-stitch each strip to hold the fold in place.

8. Stitch the length of elastic to the wrong side of the tail piece. Once you've sewn the elastic end to the fleece end, pull the elastic so it's fully stretched as it feeds through the machine. When you've finished the seam, release the tension; both the fabric and elastic will contract. To strengthen the connection, make a second reinforcing seam; pull the elastic to stretch it while you sew it a second time. Fold the tail piece in half lengthwise, right sides together (the elastic will be on the outside), and stitch 1 end and the length of the cut edges together. Turn the tail right-side out (Figure 5).

9. Place the pant backs right sides together. Insert the open end of the tail between the layers where the bottom starts to round. Pin then stitch the pant backs together down the center seam, catching the open tail end in your seam (Figure 6). Working on the wrong side, press the seam flat above and below the tail. Fold down and press ¼" (6mm) of the top pant edge.

10. Pin the body back pieces right sides together. Stitch the curved bottom side together (Figure 7). Lay the back of the pants over the back of the body, right sides up, and align the bottom edges. Pin the folded pant edge to the back; refer to the body/pant front and match the positioning. Add several pins to the center of the pant bottoms to help hold them in position. Stitch across the top edge, attaching the back of the pants to the back of the body. Make a vertical topstitched seam on either side of the back pant seam (Figure 8).

11. Fold each belt loop strip in half lengthwise, right sides together, and stitch the long edges together, leaving the short ends open. Turn the pieces right-side out and press them flat. Fold over each top and bottom end twice (to conceal the cut edges) before pinning 2 belt loops to the pant front and 3 belt loops to the pant back (keep clear of the side seams). Machine-stitch the tops and bottoms of the loops in place.

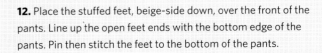

12. Place the stuffed feet, beige-side down, over the front of the pants. Line up the open feet ends with the bottom edge of the pants. Pin then stitch the feet to the bottom of the pants.

13. Lay the body front, right-side up, on your work surface. Position the 3 hair strips down over your troll's forehead (the hair ends should extend beyond the top of the head). Place the ears beige-side down over his cheeks; the flat open ends should extend out from the sides of his head. Cross the arms over the front of his body so that the open shoulder ends extend out from either side of his body.

14. Lay the back of the troll over the front, right sides together, lining up the top of the heads and the sides (Figure 9). Make sure the length of the arms (and hands) are tucked inside so they won't get caught in the seams. Pin the body back to the body front, trapping the hair, ears and shoulders between the layers. Machine-stitch around the outside edge, leaving the bottom open. Turn the body right-side out to check your

seams. Make any necessary adjustments and then turn the piece wrong-side out to make a second reinforcing seam.

15. Tuck the feet and hands down into the body. Lay the base piece right-side down over the open bottom. Pin the base piece to the bottom of the pant fronts and backs. Stitch it in place, catching the feet in the seam. Leave a 3"–4" (7.6cm–10.2cm) opening on 1 side of the back of the pants (Figure 10). Turn the troll right-side out.

16. Firmly stuff the troll with stuffing. Tuck ¼" (6mm) of the opening edges in and then hand-stitch them together with small invisible stitches.

17. Fold the length of the belt in half, right sides together, and stitch the outside edge. Use a stuffing stick to turn the belt right-side out. Feed 1 end through the belt loops, then tie the belt in a loose knot at the troll's belly. Tie each belt end into an overhand knot.

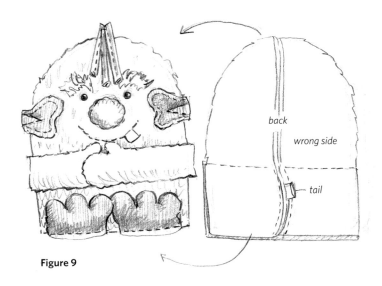

Figure 9

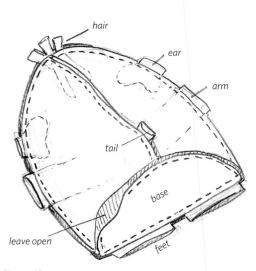

Figure 10

Puss in Boots

THIS SAUCY FELLOW is more than just a well-dressed feline. His outstretched arms and soft body make him a huggably soft companion. His stylish boots, belt, vest, collar and hat are all removable. Encourage your little one to practice dressing him to master belts, buckles and bows.

Note: Add a ¼" (6mm) seam allowance to the indicated pattern pieces.

Dimensions: 20" × 15" (50.8cm × 38.1cm) with hat

MATERIALS

Templates on pages 105, 106

½ yard (0.5m) plush felt (in desired cat color)

¼ yard (0.2m) beige fleece

Scrap of pink wool felt for nose

Wool felt in white, brown, purple and aqua blue

¼ yard (0.2m) floral printed cotton

¼ yard (0.2m) diamond printed cotton

¼ yard (0.2m) green quilting flannel

Sewing thread in coordinating colors

29" (73.7cm) of ⅝" (1.6cm) brown velvet ribbon

Two ½" (1.3cm) black safety eyes

1¾" × 1" (4.4cm × 2.5cm) buckle (from purse hardware)

Fiberfill stuffing

Fusible fleece interfacing

TOOLS

Scissors

Sewing machine

Straight pins

Iron and ironing board

Sizzix die-cut machine with 1" (2.5cm) and ⅞" (2.2cm) circle dies (or hand cut the felt eyes)

Stuffing stick

Rotary cutter

Ruler

Cutting mat

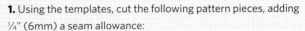

Cat

1. Using the templates, cut the following pattern pieces, adding ¼" (6mm) a seam allowance:

- From the plush felt, cut 2 cat faces, 2 cat backs, 2 cat ears (flip the template to cut 1 in reverse), 4 cat arms (cut 2 in reverse) and 4 cat legs (cut 2 in reverse).
- From the fleece, cut 1 cat belly, 2 cat ears (cut 1 in reverse) and 2 cat tails (cut 1 in reverse).
- From pink felt, cut a ½" (1.3cm) circle.

2. Placing right sides together, pin and seam the top edge of the face pieces together. Fold the belly piece in half, right sides together, and place the center top between the head pieces. Make 2 separate seams to connect the bottom edge of the head pieces to the top edge of the belly piece (Figure 1).

3. To make the eyes, die or hand cut two 1" (2.5cm) aqua blue felt circles and two ⅞" (2.2cm) white felt circles. Cut a small slit in the center of each felt circle. Insert the screw end of a safety eye into a white circle then an aqua circle. Repeat the process with the second eye and remaining circles.

Make small slits on both sides of the plush felt head, then insert the screw end of the eyes into the holes. Working on the back side of the head, slide a plastic backing piece up each screw end until it rests snugly against the underside of the eyes (Figure 2).

Hand-stitch the nose in place where the 2 face pieces connect to the belly piece. Make small, invisible stitches that sink into the felt.

4. Stitch the ears: With right sides together, pair a fleece ear with each plush ear, making a right and left ear, then stitch around the outside edge, keeping the bottom edge open. Trim the excess fabric from the tips and turn the ears right-side out (Figure 3).

5. Pairing right sides together, pin the arms, legs and tail pieces together, creating right and left arms and legs. Machine-stitch around the outside of each pair, leaving the flat ends unsewn. Use a stuffing stick to turn the pieces right-side out. Use your tool again to push stuffing down into the hands, feet and tail ends first before filling the rest of the limbs and tail.

6. Place the cat backs right sides together. Insert the open end of the stuffed tail between the layers at the center seam; the open end should extend beyond the fabric edges. Refer to the pattern for exact placement. Stitch from the head down the back and to the base, catching the open tail end in your seam (Figure 4).

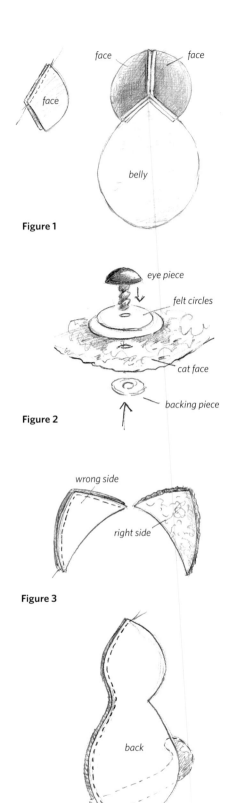

Figure 1

Figure 2

Figure 3

Figure 4

7. Placing right sides together, pin the cat back to the cat front. Insert the ears and arms between the layers, letting the open ends extend beyond the edges of the body pieces; pin in place. Stitch from the bottom edge up 1 side, around the head and back down the other side, leaving the entire bottom edge open (Figure 5). Check your seam to make sure the ears and arms are all securely attached; make any necessary adjustments.

8. Turn the cat right-side out and then stuff the head and belly. Tuck in the fabric edges at the bottom of the cat. Insert the legs into the opening, pointing the toes to the front (Figure 6). Hand-stitch the legs to the bottom of the cat's body, making sure your stitches sink into the plush felt while sewing the bottom closed.

Hat

1. Using the templates, cut the following pattern pieces, adding a ¼" (6mm) seam allowance:
- From the aqua blue felt, cut 2 hat sides and 1 hat top.
- From the purple felt, cut 2 hat sides and 1 hat top.
- From the white felt, cut 2 feathers. Do not add a seam allowance.

2. Placing right sides together, seam the aqua hat top to the top edge of both aqua hat sides. Once you've connected the aqua sides to the aqua hat top, repeat the process with the purple pieces.

3. Keeping right sides together, fold the aqua hat top in half to flatten it. Make 2 separate seams to stitch the aqua hat sides together. Repeat the process with the purple hat.

4. Turn the purple hat right-side out and place it inside the aqua hat, so that both right sides are together (Figure 7). Line up the front and back seams of both hats and pin them together so they don't shift while you stitch. Make a continuous seam around the hat brim, starting at the center back seam and ending 1½" (3.8cm) short of your starting point (Figure 8).

5. Pull the hat right-side out through the opening. Fit the aqua hat lining inside the purple hat. Tuck in the edges at the brim opening and make small stitches to hand-sew it closed.

6. Stack the 2 white felt feather pieces together and make a seam up and down the center to connect the layers. Pin the feather so it extends at a jaunty diagonal angle out the top of the hat. Working on the underside of the feather, hand stitch the center seam to the outside of the hat.

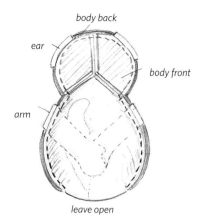

body back
ear
body front
arm
leave open

Figure 5

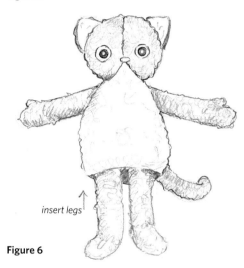

insert legs

Figure 6

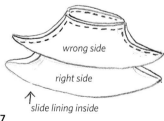

wrong side
right side
slide lining inside

Figure 7

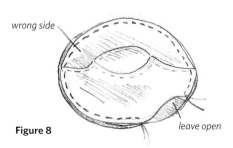

wrong side
leave open

Figure 8

Collar

1. Cut a 2½" × 24" (6.4cm × 61cm) rectangle from the white felt. Fold the collar in half and use the collar template as your guide to cut 1 side into scallops.

2. Fold and stitch pleats to ruffle the felt collar. Begin the collar with a ½" (1.3cm) fold, then make 9 more ½" (1.3cm) pleats spaced 1" (2.5cm) apart down the length of the felt. End the collar with another ½" (1.3cm) pleat, for a total of 11 folds. Pin the pleats along the straight edge, leaving the scalloped side open. Make a seam ½" (1.3cm) from the straight edge down the length of the collar. Catch the pleats in your seam and remove the pins as you stitch.

3. Position the collar in the center of the brown velvet ribbon, with the ribbon extended evenly on either side. Fold and pin the width of the ribbon around the seamed collar. Machine-stitch the folded ribbon edges and sandwiched felt in a single seam.

Vest

1. Use the templates and add a ¼" (6mm) seam allowance when you cut the following pattern pieces:

- From the flannel, cut 1 left vest front, 1 right vest front and 1 vest back.
- From the floral cotton, cut 1 left vest front, 1 right vest front and 1 vest back (linings).

2. With right sides together, place the flannel vest fronts over the flannel back piece. Pin the shoulder and side edges together. Make separate seams to stitch the shoulders and sides together, being sure to leave the collar, armholes and base unattached. Working on the wrong side, iron the seams open and flat. Repeat the process for the floral cotton lining pieces.

3. Placing right sides together, pin the edges of the cotton lining to the flannel. Make sure you line up the shoulder and side seams. Make a continuous seam around the outside edge of the vest, leaving the armholes unsewn (Figure 9). Trim excess fabric from the corners and shoulders, then turn the vest right-side out through 1 of the armholes.

4. Iron the lined vest flat, then tuck in ¼" (6mm) of fabric around the armholes. Pin the ironed and folded armhole edges together. Topstitch around the armhole openings and then around the seamed outside edge of the vest (Figure 10).

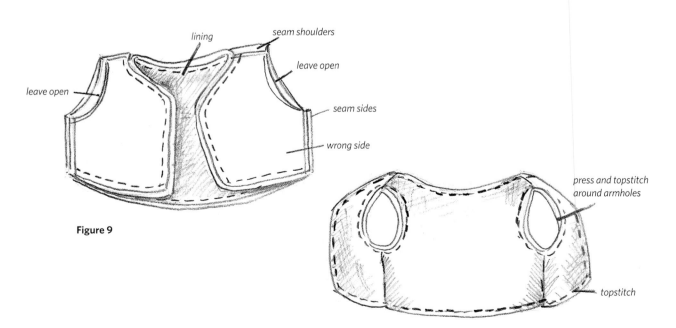

lining

seam shoulders

leave open

leave open

seam sides

wrong side

Figure 9

press and topstitch around armholes

topstitch

Figure 10

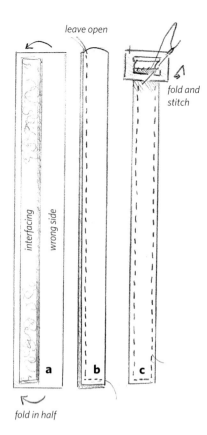

leave open

interfacing

wrong side

fold and stitch

a b c

fold in half

Figure 11 (a, b and c)

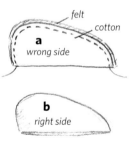

felt

cotton

a
wrong side

b
right side

Figure 12 (a and b)

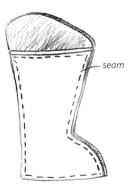

seam

Figure 13

Belt

1. Use a rotary cutter, ruler and cutting mat to cut a 3½" × 20½" (8.9cm × 52.1cm) strip of cotton diamond fabric. Then cut a 1½" × 20½" (3.8cm × 52.1cm) strip of interfacing.

2. Fuse the interfacing down the length of the fabric strip: Working on the wrong side of the fabric, position the strip a ¼" (6mm) from the bottom edge, then iron it in place, following the manufacturer's instructions (Figure 11a).

3. Placing right sides together, fold and pin the strip in half lengthwise. Working ¼" (6mm) from the outside edge, stitch 1 short end, turn the corner and stitch the length, leaving the second short end open (Figure 11b). Trim excess fabric from the corners and turn the belt right-side out through the open short end.

4. Iron the belt flat, then topstitch the belt ¼" (6mm) from the seamed edge. Wrap the open belt end around the center of the buckle, tucking under the unfinished end before pinning it to the belt. Hand-stitch the folded and pinned belt end, securing the buckle in place (Figure 11c).

Boots

1. Use the templates and add a ¼" (6mm) seam allowance as you cut the following pattern pieces:
- From the brown felt, cut 4 boot sides and 4 boot tops.
- From the cotton diamond fabric, cut 4 boot tops (flip the template and cut 2 boot tops in reverse).

2. Placing right sides together, pair a felt boot top with each cotton boot top for 4 sets, making sure you have both left and right boots. Working with 1 set at a time, machine-stitch up 1 rounded side, across the top and down the other rounded side, leaving the flat bottom edge unsewn (Figure 12a). Turn each seamed boot top right-side out and iron flat (Figure 12b).

3. Pairing felt sides together, pin the straight edge of the boot top to the boot side. The taller end of the boot top should line up with the heel side of the boot side. Machine stitch the tops in place for both boots.

4. Placing right sides together (seamed sides on the outside), pin the edges of the boot sides together. Make a continuous seam down the back of the boot side, across the bottom of the foot, and back up the front of the boot (Figure 13). Repeat the process with the second boot. Turn both boots right-side out.

The Little Mermaid

HAPPIEST ONSHORE OR AWASH IN A SEA OF BED COVERS, this mermaid is perfectly scaled to fit in your child's arms. Her soft body is sewn with patterned and sequined linen, but her hair is styled with rosy hues of felt. The ruched ribbon bikini can be removed and retied in place.

 Note: Pattern pieces include a ¼" (6mm) seam allowance.

Dimensions: 14" × 11" (35.6cm × 27.9cm)

MATERIALS

Templates on page 107

¼ yard (0.2m) yard off-white linen

¼ yard (0.2m) turquoise sequined linen

⅛ yard (0.1m) flowered linen

Wool felt in red, peach and chartreuse

Two ¼" (6mm) black safety eyes

Embroidery floss in red and black

27" (68.6cm) of 1" (2.5cm) blue sheer organdy ribbon

Fusible fleece interfacing

Fiberfill stuffing

Sewing thread in coordinating colors

TOOLS

Sewing machine

Scissors

Straight pins

Embroidery and sewing needles

Iron and ironing board

Sizzix die-cut machine with flower die cut (or purchase precut flowers in the button section of your fabric store)

Stuffing stick

Rotary cutter

Ruler

Cutting mat

1. Using the templates, cut the following pattern pieces:
- From the off-white linen, cut 2 body pieces and 4 arms (flip the template and cut 2 arms in reverse).
- From the interfacing, cut a lining piece for each body and arm piece ¼" (6mm) smaller than the pattern.
- From the turquoise linen, cut 2 tail pieces.
- From the red felt, cut the front and back hair pieces and 2 hair buns. Fold 1 bun piece and cut the marked X in the center.

2. Adhere the linings to the wrong side of each body and arm piece. Follow the manufacturer's instructions to iron the linings to the linen fabric. The lining pieces are inset so they won't add bulk to the seams (Figure 1).

3. Pin the front hair piece to the top of the front body piece. Contour stitch a single seam along the bottom edge. Pin the back hair piece over the head portion of the back body piece. Make a single seam along the bottom edge (Figure 2).

4. Snip 2 tiny holes on the face under the bangs for the eyes, then insert the screw end of the safety eyes through the openings. On the wrong side, slide a plastic backing piece on each screw end until it rests snugly against the interfacing.

Use 3 strands of black embroidery floss to make an ⅛" (3mm) V-stitch on the outside of each eye. Make a diagonal ½" (1.3cm) eyebrow over each eye.

Use 3 strands of red floss to make the mouth. Make 3 connected ¼" (6mm) stitches: a flat center stitch between 2 angled stitches. (See template for placement.)

5. Pair up the arms and pin them right sides together. Machine-stitch around the outside edge, leaving the shoulder end open. Turn the arms right-side out and stuff them lightly with fiberfill (Figure 3).

6. Position and cross the arms over the front body piece, lining up the open shoulder ends with the insertion markings on the pattern. Machine-stitch the ends closed while attaching them to the body (Figure 4).

Figure 1

Figure 2

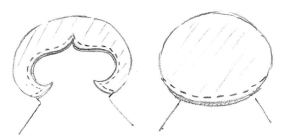

Figure 3

Figure 4   **Figure 5**

7. Placing right sides together, pin the top of a tail piece to the bottom of each body piece. Machine-stitch them together (Figure 5). Press the seam flat.

8. Using 3 strands of black floss, make an ⅛" (3mm) V-stitch belly button just above the tail on the front body piece.

9. Pin the front and back body pieces right sides together. Be sure the arms are tucked inside and won't interfere with the seaming. Machine-stitch around the outside edge switching thread colors between the body and tail. Leave a 2" (5.1cm) opening under 1 arm or along the tail to turn your mermaid right-side out (Figure 6).

10. Stuff your mermaid, pushing stuffing up into the head and down into the tail points first, then fill the rest of her body. Stuff her completely; understuffed dolls will become floppy. Match the thread color and hand-stitch the opening closed.

11. Pin the 2 bun pieces together and machine-stitch around the outside edge. Turn the bun right-side out through the cut X. Push stuffing into the opening to fill the bun. Hand-stitch the bun to the top of the back of the head (Figure 7).

12. Using a rotary cutter, ruler and cutting mat, cut 3 peach and 6 red ½" × 24" (1.3cm × 61cm) felt strips for the hair. Stack the 9 hair strips and begin braiding them 6" (15.2cm) from the end in 3 groups of 3 felt strips. Continue braiding for 12" (30.5cm). Let the remaining 6" (15.2cm) hang loose. Hand-stitch the beginning and end of the braid to stop it from unraveling (Figure 8).

Wrap the braided portion of the hair around the bun and let the unbraided strips hang down below the bun. Hand stitch the braid to the bun (Figure 9).

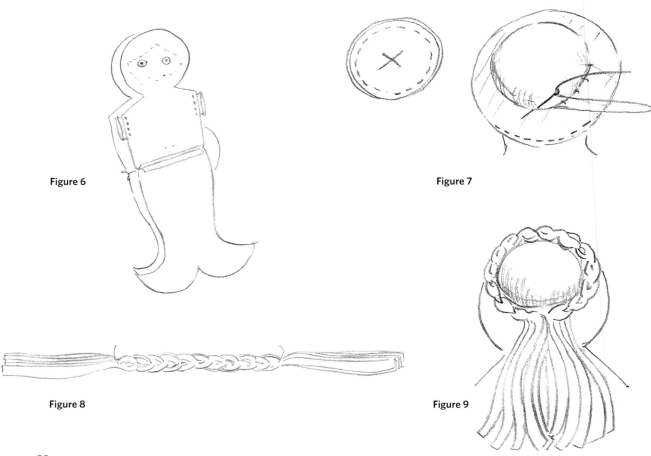

Figure 6

Figure 7

Figure 8

Figure 9

13. Cut felt flowers and use them to embellish the finished hair. You'll need 5 large flowers and 5 smaller flower inserts. Follow your die-cut machine instructions to cut them out of peach and chartreuse felt (or buy precut flowers). Arrange the flowers around the base of the bun, then hand-stitch with red embroidery floss through each flower center (Figure 10).

14. Using a rotary cutter, ruler and cutting mat, cut two 2½" × 26" (6.4cm × 66cm) strips from the flowered linen for the bikini top. Working on the wrong side of the fabric, fold and press ¼" (6mm) edge on all 4 sides of each strip. Fold again on 1 long edge and 2 short edges, and repeat with the second strip.

15. Machine-stitch the double-folded edges on 1 strip. Increase your stitch length to make a gathering seam along the long single-folded edge. Gently pull the thread on either side to gather the strip until it measures 8" (20.3cm) at the top. Repeat with the second strip (Figure 11).

16. Pin the gathered edge of 1 strip to the top of the organdy ribbon; let 9" (22.9cm) of ribbon extend out either side of the fabric. Machine-stitch the gathered fabric to the ribbon. Repeat the process to attach the second gathered strip to the bottom of the ribbon (Figure 12). Tie the finished ribbon bikini around the mermaid's chest.

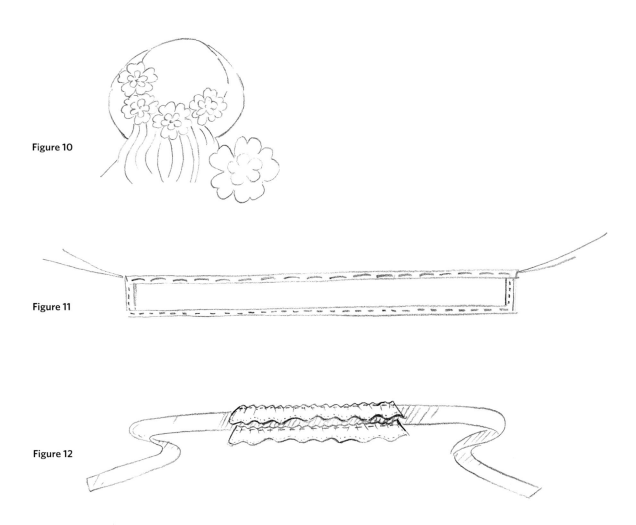

Figure 10

Figure 11

Figure 12

Little Red Riding Hood and the Wolf

AMAZINGLY EASY TO SEW, this two-sided doll will spark imaginative play. At first glance, the darling Red Riding Hood looks like a simple doll— but swing the cape around to the other side to reveal the mischievous wolf. A length of elastic and a hook-and-loop dot are the only special effects you need to create the clever moveable cape.

Note: Pattern pieces include a ¼" (6mm) seam allowance. Felt detail pieces are top stitched ⅛" (3mm) from the raw edges.

Dimensions: 13½" × 8" (34.3cm × 20.3cm)

MATERIALS

Templates on pages 108, 109

¼ yard (0.2m) red printed cotton

¼ yard (0.2m) pink printed cotton

Wool felt in flesh tone, dark-brown, red, aqua,
   light-gray, dark-gray, pink, white and black

Fusible web

8" (20.3cm) red rickrack

10" (25.4cm) pink pompom trim

Two ¼" (6mm) black safety eyes (for doll)

Two ⅜" (1cm) black safety eyes (for wolf)

11" (27.9cm) length of ¼" (6mm) black elastic

Sewing thread in coordinating colors

Embroidery floss in black and red

1" (2.5cm) hook-and-loop fastener dot

Fiberfill stuffing

TOOLS

Sewing machine

Scissors

Embroidery and sewing needles

Straight pins

Iron and ironing board

Die-cut machine with flower die cut and ⅞" (2.2cm)
   and ⅜" (1cm) circle dies (or purchase precut
   flowers in the button section of your fabric store
   and cut the circles by hand)

Red Riding Hood side

1. Beginning with the Red Riding Hood side, use the templates to
cut the following pattern pieces:

- From the flesh-tone felt, cut 1 body piece.
- Follow the manufacturer's instructions to iron the fusible
  web to the wrong side of the pink printed cotton, then cut
  the dress out of the prepared fabric.
- From the aqua felt, cut the shawl; from the brown felt, cut
  the hair; and from the red felt, cut the hat and flower (if
  using die-cut machine).
- From the pink felt, cut two ⅞" (2.2cm) circles (cheeks), and
  from the white felt, cut one ⅜" (1cm) circle (flower center).

2. Remove the paper backing from the fusible web side of the
dress, position the fabric over the lower half of the body piece
and iron it in place. Pin the aqua shawl over the top of the dress
and machine-stitch along the top felt edge.

   Pin the pompom trim along the bottom edge of the shawl so
that it extends beyond the fabric edges on either side. Machine-
stitch the flat portion of the trim in place. Pin the rickrack along
the bottom edge of the dress, letting it extend beyond the fabric
edges. Machine-stitch down the center of the red rickrack,
catching the bottom edge of the dress in the seam.

3. Place the hat over the top of the body piece, then tuck the hair
piece under the hat so that the hair frames the face.

   Machine-stitch the bottom edge of the hat, then switch
thread colors and contour stitch the bottom edge of the hair.
Pin the pink felt circle cheeks to either side of the face, leaving
room for the eyes and mouth. Hand-stitch the outside edges
of the cheeks in place. Use tiny stitches so that they sink into
the felt and become invisible. (Placement of details is noted on
template.)

4. Snip 2 tiny holes under the bangs for the eyes, then insert the
screw end of the ¼" (6mm) safety eyes through the openings.
On the wrong side of the doll, slide a plastic backing piece onto
each screw end until it rests snugly against the fabric.

   Using 6 strands of black embroidery floss, make a ¼" (6mm)
V-stitch on the outside of each eye for the eyelashes. Using
6 strands of red floss, make the mouth with 3 connected ½"
(1.3cm) stitches: a flat center stitch between 2 angled stitches.
To give her fuller lips, intersect the center of the middle stitch
with a ¼" (6mm) V-stitch.

5. Use the templates to cut the following pattern pieces for the Wolf side:
- From the light-gray felt, cut 1 body.
- From the white felt, cut 1 face and 1 chest piece.
- From the dark-gray felt, cut 1 forehead and 1 pair of legs.
- From the black felt, cut 1 tail and 1 nose.
- From the printed red cotton, cut 4 cape pieces.

6. Arrange and pin the following on the gray body piece: Lay the forehead over the white face, then position the black nose over the end of the forehead. Lay the white chest over the legs, then tuck the tail under the feet. Machine-stitch around the outside edge of each piece, using coordinating thread. Stitch the bottom layers in place first. Unpin and lift the chest, nose and paws out of the way then reposition them when you are ready to stitch the top layers.

7. For the wolf's eyes, snip 2 tiny holes in the white felt on either side of the nose. Insert the screw end of the ³⁄₈" (1cm) safety eyes through the openings. On the wrong side of the wolf, slide a plastic backing piece onto each screw end until it rests snugly against the fabric. Use 6 strands of black embroidery floss to create five ¼" (6mm) stitches for the mouth. The stitches should form a connected *W*.

8. Pin 2 cape pieces right sides together. Stitch around the outside edge, leaving a gap for the elastic insertion as marked on the pattern and a 1½" (3.8cm) opening along the bottom edge (Figure 1a). Repeat with remaining 2 cape pieces.

Turn the cape pieces right-side out through the bottom edge opening. Iron the sewn pieces flat, tucking in the openings so they mimic the seamed edges. Top stitch as marked on the template, closing the bottom openings but leaving the elastic openings clear (Figure 1b). Lay the finished cape halves side by side, then thread the elastic through the openings.

Wolf Side

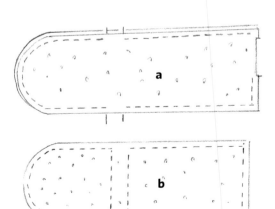

Figure 1 (a and b)

9. Make multiple hand-stitches of black thread to ensure the elastic ends are sewn securely onto the center of Red Riding Hood's neck, adjusting the elastic so that it won't be twisted when flipped to the wolf side. Cover your stitches with a felt flower (die-cut or bought) and a white felt center (Figure 2).

10. Pile the elastic and cape halves over Red Riding Hood's middle, so they won't be caught in side seams. Pin pompoms at the side edges out of the way, or clip off excess pompom if it falls in the stitch line. Lay her facedown over the wolf and pin the edges together. Machine-stitch the outside edges together, leaving a 2" (5.1cm) opening near the base (Figure 3). Turn the doll right-side out.

11. Pull the elastic over the top of the connected head, so it falls under the wolf's chin. The cape halves should fall to either side of the doll. Firmly stuff the doll starting with the pointed head and working your way down to the base. Hand-stitch the opening closed.

12. Use black thread to hand-stitch the elastic where it falls in the center of the wolf's neck. Leave the rest of the elastic unsewn so the cape can swing easily from one side to the other.

Lay the hood portions of the cape halves over the wolf's head. Mark where the 2 pieces overlap and hand-sew a female hook-and-loop fastener dot to one side and a male fastener dot to the other side. The connection will work when the hood is reversed to cover the wolf's face (Figure 4).

Figure 3

Figure 4

Figure 2

Unicorn

I'M CONVINCED THAT EVERY GIRL has a phase when she is obsessed with unicorns. Magical horses with luminous moonlit bodies set the stage for imaginative adventures. I chose chenille for the body for cuddly softness. The long mane and tail are quickly sewn up with no-fray fleece. If you add pellets to weight the feet, the finished unicorn can stand guard until its child returns.

Note: Add ¼" (6mm) seam allowances to the indicated pattern pieces only.

MATERIALS

Templates on page 110

½ yard (0.5m) purple printed cotton

1 yard (0.9m) white chenille

½ yard (0.5m) purple fleece

Sewing thread in off-white

Embroidery floss in black

Fiberfill stuffing

Plastic pellets

TOOLS

Sewing machine

Scissors

Embroidery and sewing needles

Straight pins

Stuffing stick

Paper (for making funnel)

Measuring cups

Dimensions: 23" × 21" (58.4cm × 53.3cm)

1. Use the templates to cut the following pattern pieces:
- From the chenille, cut 2 body pieces (flip the template and cut 1 in reverse), 2 ears and 1 head insert.
- From the purple printed cotton, cut 3 horn pieces (add seam allowance), 2 ears (add seam allowance), 2 undersides (add seam allowance; cut 1 in reverse), 2 front legs (cut 1 in reverse) and 2 back legs (cut 1 in reverse).
- From the purple fleece, cut one 12" × 20" (30.5cm × 50.8cm) rectangle for the mane and one 24" × 15" (61cm × 38.1cm) rectangle for the tail.

2. To make the horn, place right sides together, pin the outside edges, and then machine-stitch 3 separate seams to connect the pieces. Trim the excess fabric off the tip and turn the horn right-side out. Use a stuffing stick to push stuffing up to the horn tip first, then fill the rest of the horn (Figure 1).

3. To make the ears, pair and pin a cotton ear to each chenille ear, right sides together. Stitch around the outside edge of each pair, leaving the flat bottom edge open. Trim the extra fabric from the tip, then turn the ears right-side out (Figure 2).

4. Placing right sides together, pin the top edge of the front leg to the rounded inset of the underside. Pin the angled top portion of the back leg to the angled end of the underside. The rest of the back leg will extend beyond the underside piece. Stitch the legs to the underside. Repeat the process with the second set of legs and second underside.

Placing right sides together, pin the tops of the undersides together, then pin the straight tops of the 2 back legs together. Make a single seam across the top edge to join the undersides and back legs together (Figure 3). This step stabilizes the legs; a single unseamed piece doesn't work as effectively.

5. Stack the body pieces right sides together, positioning the cotton undersides between the body's chenille legs. Pin each pair of cotton and chenille legs together. Draw the front of the underside up between the body's chest and pin it in place.

6. Insert the ears, tip sides down, between the foreheads and head insert. The cotton sides should rest against the chenille body pieces, and the chenille sides against the insert. Pin the insert in place, catching the ends of the ears between the layers. Continue pinning the edges of the neck, head and back together. Start your seam at the chest just above the underside edge. Stitch your way up and around the nose. When you reach the insert at the forehead, stitch around 1 side first, catching the ear in your seam.

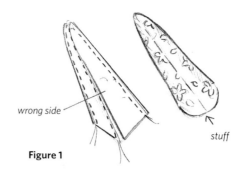

wrong side *stuff*

Figure 1

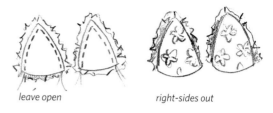

leave open *right-sides out*

Figure 2

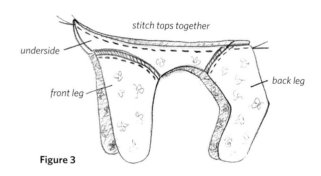

stitch tops together *underside* *front leg* *back leg*

Figure 3

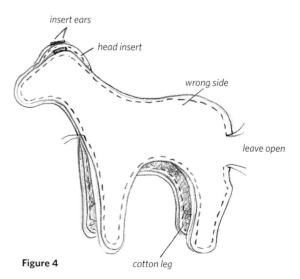

insert ears *head insert* *wrong side* *leave open* *cotton leg*

Figure 4

Repeat the process on the other side of the insert. Starting at the end of the insert, stitch down the neck and back, leaving a 5" (12.7cm) opening before you reach the underside.

Overlapping with the seam on the neck, sew down around 1 set of front legs, across the belly and around 1 set of back legs. Stop at the bottom of the 5" (12.7cm) opening. Repeat on the other side (Figure 4). Check your seams, trim away excess fabric and turn the unicorn right-side out.

7. Fill the feet with pellets, then fill the rest of the body with polyester stuffing. Pour a half cup (4 oz) of pellets down into each foot. Roll paper into a funnel to help feed the pellets down the leg. Switch to polyester stuffing to fill the rest of the legs. Next, stuff the nose, head, neck and body.

8. Fold the fleece mane in half, then stitch up and down the width of the folded mane in 1 continuous seam. The folded edge will stay connected and will later attach to the unicorn; the open edge will be cut apart.

Starting at 1 end, make a vertical seam from the folded edge to the open edge. Once you reach the open edge, switch your direction and make a ¼" (6mm) horizontal seam before making a vertical seam back up to the folded edge. Continue working this way until the entire mane has been stitched.

Cut the fleece apart at the open edge between each pair of seams; leave the folded edge connected. Repeat the process for the tail, increasing the length of the seams to match the length of the tail (Figure 5).

9. Hand-stitch the base of the horn to the head insert between the ears. Fold the mane in half widthwise, then lay and pin the folded edge between the horn and the base of the neck. Hand stitch the (connected) edge to the chenille neck (Figure 6). Roll the connected tail edge and insert it into the rump opening. Stitch the around the tail to secure it in place, then tuck in the chenille edges and sew the remaining opening closed (Figure 7).

10. Use 6 strands of black floss and an embroidery needle to make the eyes, nostrils and mouth. Each eye a ½" (1.3cm) V-stitch. Each nostril is a a single ¼" (6mm) stitch. Make 4 connected ½" (1.3cm) stitches under the snout to make a slightly smiling mouth.

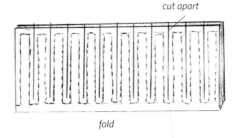

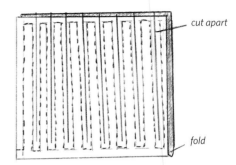

Figure 5

Figure 6

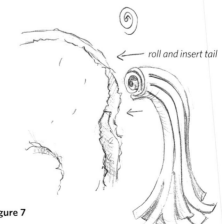

Figure 7

Shoemaker's Elves

EVERYONE NEEDS A PAIR OF ELF HELPERS that magically arrive in the middle of the night and stitch up your unfinished projects. Although, sewing up miniature felt hats, aprons, vests and pointed shoes is not work, but a whimsical delight! Once decked in all their finery, this happy pair of helpers could play roles in many different imaginary tales.

 Note: Do not add seam allowances to the tempates.

Dimensions: 8" × 6" (20.3cm × 15.2cm)

MATERIALS

Templates on page 111

Wool felt in light-tan, light-orange, light-blue, medium-blue, aqua, lime green, brown, dark-orange and tan

Embroidery floss in black, light-tan, green, mustard, light-blue, orange and red

Fiberfill stuffing

TOOLS

Scissors

Embroidery and sewing needles

Straight pins

Stuffing stick

Girl Elf

1. Use the templates to cut the following pattern pieces:

- From the light-tan felt, cut 2 body pieces and 4 arms.
- From the aqua felt, cut 2 dress pieces.
- From the lime green felt, cut 2 dress trim pieces and 1 bow.
- From the light-blue felt, cut 4 legs.
- From the medium-blue felt, cut 1 hat front, 1 hat back and 1 heart.
- From the dark-orange felt, cut 1 front hair piece and 2 back hair pieces.
- From the light-orange felt, cut 1 apron and 1 bow.

2. Arrange the front hair piece on the top of the front body piece. Using 3 strands of orange floss, stitch the bottom edge of the hair to the front body piece (Figure 1). Place the 2 back hair pieces over the body back and stitch the bottom edges in place.

3. Using 3 strands of black floss, make 2 inverted Vs for the eyes. Each stitch should be ¼" (6mm) long. Add angled ⅛" (3mm) stitches to either side of the eyes for eyelashes. Using 3 strands of light-tan floss, make a small V-stitch for the nose. Switch to 3 strands of red floss to make a slightly larger V-stitch mouth (Figure 1).

4. Pin a dress piece to the body front and the second dress piece to the body back. Using 3 strands of lime green floss, make small straight stitches across the top edge of the shirt collar. Tuck the dress trim under the bottom edge of the dress and pin it in place (Figure 1).

5. Pin the leg pieces together, then begin stitching the outside edges together with 3 strands of light-blue floss. Make small, closely spaced straight stitches. Leave the tops open and unsewn (Figure 2).

   Pin the arm pieces together, and use 3 strands of light-tan floss to whipstitch the outside edges together. Leave the shoulder ends open and unsewn. Using a stuffing stick, push small amounts of stuffing into the toes and hands first, then fill completely (Figure 3).

Figure 1

Figure 2

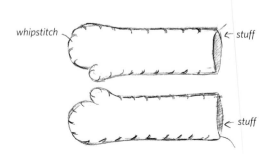

Figure 3

6. With right sides facing out, stack the front piece over the back piece. Insert the shoulders of the arms between the layers, about ¼" (6mm) down from the neck of the dress; pin the sides together, trapping the arms in place.

Insert the top of the legs between the center bottom of the dress; the feet should face forward. Pin the bottom edges of the dress, trapping the legs and dress trim between the layers (Figure 4).

7. Using 3 strands of lime green floss, make small straight stitches down 1 side of the dress, across the bottom and up the other side. Go slowly, making sure you catch the arms, legs and dress trim in your seam.

8. Push stuffing into the base of the connected dress, then fill the rest of the chest up to the neck. Using 3 strands of light-tan floss, whipstitch the sides of the head and ears together.

9. Add more stuffing to the neck, then fill the head. Using 3 strands of orange floss, whipstitch around 1 pigtail, over the top of the head and back down around the second pigtail (Figure 5).

10. Lay the hat front over the hat back. Using 3 strands of light-blue floss, make straight stitches around the outside edge. Stitch the center of the bow to 1 side of the hat with 3 strands of mustard floss. Slip the finished hat over the elf's head.

11. Center the heart in the middle of the apron. Stitch around the outside edge of the heart with 3 strands of orange floss. Lay the apron around the doll's middle. Place the orange bow over the ends of the apron ties, and attach the entire piece to the elf with straight stiches using 3 strands of lime green floss.

Boy Elf

1. Use the templates to cut the following pattern pieces:
- From the light-tan felt, cut 2 body pieces and 4 arms.
- From the light-orange felt, cut 2 shirt pieces.
- From the medium-blue felt, cut 4 legs.
- From the aqua felt, cut 2 hat pieces.
- From the lime green felt, cut 1 feather.
- From the brown felt, cut 1 hair front and 1 hair back.
- From the tan felt, cut 2 vest fronts and 1 vest back.

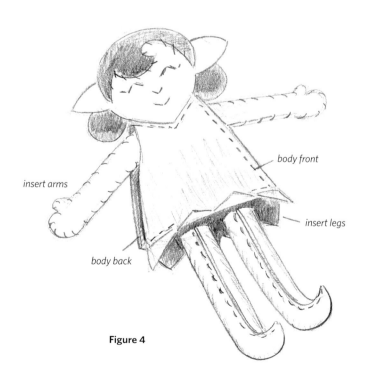

insert arms

body front

insert legs

body back

Figure 4

hand-stitch head closed

stuff

Figure 5

2. Arrange the front hair piece on top of the front body piece. Using 3 strands of black floss, whipstitch the bottom edge of the hair to the front body piece. Place the back hair piece over the body back and whipstitch the bottom edges in place (Figure 6).

3. Follow Step 3 of the girl elf instructions to embroider the face, omitting the eyelashes (Figure 6).

4. Follow Step 4 of the girl elf instructions, replacing dress pieces with shirt pieces and using mustard floss. With 3 strands of lime green floss, make 2 cross-stitches in the center front of the shirt (Figure 6).

5. Follow Step 5 of the girl elf instructions to pin, stitch and stuff the arms and legs.

6. Follow Step 6 of the girl elf instructions to pin the body pieces, referring to his shirt instead of her dress.

7. Follow Step 7 of the girl elf instructions, using 3 strands of mustard floss to stitch together the body pieces.

8. Follow Step 8 of the girl elf instructions to stuff the body and stitch the ears and sides of the head.

9. Add more stuffing to the neck and then fill the head. Using 3 strands of brown floss, whipstitch together the hair and the top of the head.

10. Stack the hat pieces together. Fold and pin up ½" (1.3cm) on the front and back of the straight side. Using 3 strands of lime green floss, make small, straight stitches around the outside edge, catching the upturned felt in the seam. Use 3 strands of orange floss to stitch the feather to the front of the hat (Figure 7). Slip the hat over the elf's head.

11. Stack the vest fronts over the vest back, and pin the shoulder and side seams together. Using 3 strands of mustard floss, make 4 separate, small straight-stitched seams, 1 along each shoulder and 1 along each side (Figure 8). Dress the elf in his vest.

Figure 6

fold up

Figure 7

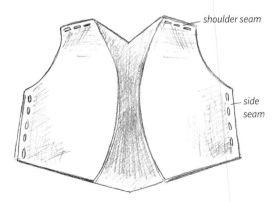

shoulder seam

side seam

Figure 8

Ugly Duckling Embroidery

A FLUFFY CYGNET (A YOUNG SWAN) regally looks on as gossipy ducklings cause a ruckus on the water. Simply cut the templates out of felt and layer them over stretched fabric. With just a few easy embroidery stitches, you'll be rewarded with an irresistibly cute creation. Gather the fabric edges to tuck them behind the needlework, and your playful pond scene is ready to be displayed in the hoop.

 Note: Use embroidery stitches to attach the felt pieces; no seam allowances are added.

Dimensions: 6" (15.2cm)

MATERIALS

Templates on page 112

6" (15.2cm) embroidery hoop

10" (25.4cm) square heavyweight muslin or linen

Wool felt in light-blue, dark-blue, yellow, gray, light-orange, dark-brown and orange

Embroidery floss in white, yellow, mustard, green, light-blue and black

Sewing thread (optional)

TOOLS

Scissors

Straight pins

Embroidery and sewing needles

Iron and ironing board

Sewing needle (optional)

1. Iron the muslin if it has wrinkles. Unscrew the outer hoop to loosen the tension and pull out the inner hoop. Place the inner hoop flat on your work surface. Center the muslin over the hoop. Line up the weave of the fabric so that the vertical threads run up and down the center of the hoop and the horizontal threads run across the middle of the hoop. With the screw at the center top, push the outer hoop down over the inner hoop trapping the fabric between the hoops. Tighten the screw to hold the fabric in place. Tug the top and bottom fabric edges followed by the right edge and left and tighten the screw once again. This will pull the fabric taut while preventing the weave from becoming distorted.

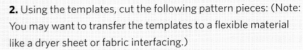

2. Using the templates, cut the following pattern pieces: (Note: You may want to transfer the templates to a flexible material like a dryer sheet or fabric interfacing.)

- From gray felt, cut the cygnet body and wing.
- From yellow felt, cut the ducklings and their wings.
- From dark-brown felt, cut the cygnet's bill.
- From orange felt, cut the ducklings' bills.
- From light-blue felt, cut the water.
- From dark-blue felt, cut the stones.
- From light-orange felt, cut the cattails.

3. Arrange the felt pieces on the muslin, using the placement diagram on the next page as a guide. Start with the largest pieces, then tuck the smaller pieces over, under and around. Layered pieces build depth and make the image appear more lifelike.

First, place the water 1" (2.5cm) from the bottom edge of the hoop. Set the blue stones in the water openings. Float the flat bottoms of the cygnet and duckling bodies on top of the water, using the placement diagram as a guide. Position the wings over all 3 birds, placing the middle duckling's second wing behind his chest. Continue placing the pieces until you're pleased with the arrangement, then pin all the pieces in place so they won't shift.

4. Using 3 strands of thread (unless otherwise noted) and the placement diagram, begin stitching. Always begin and end a new thread behind your work. It's best to use 1 color of floss in an area before moving to the next. This will help prevent spanning long stitches of floss back and forth behind your work. Remove the straight pin after you've sewn a piece in place; if a piece is especially tiny, it may be easier to hold it in place with your fingertip while you stitch.

White: Make ¼" (6mm) whipstitches around the outside edge of the cygnet's body. End your floss by making 2 straight stitches to define the end of the cygnet's wing.

Yellow: Repeat the ¼" (6mm) whipstitches around both ducklings.

Mustard: Make 2 straight stitches in the end of the middle duckling's wings to tack them in place. Make 3 stitches to do the same in the end duckling's wings; stitches increase in size from ⅛" (3mm) to ¼" (6mm). Make tiny stitches to tack down the cattail sides. Use a single strand of mustard floss and invisible stitches to tack down the orange bills.

Black: Make a French knot eye in the center of all 3 birds' heads. Use a single strand of black floss to stitch down the cygnet's bill.

Light-Blue: Make a series of straight horizontal stitches for the water. Intersperse stitches of different lengths: ¼" (6mm), ½" (1.3cm) and ¾" (1.9cm). Refer to the diagram for placement, spreading out the stitches so that the felt is tacked in place. Use a single strand of light-blue floss and small stitches to tack down the blue rocks.

Green: Make 3 blades of grass that extend from the muslin into the left rock with straight stitches about ¼" (6mm) to ½" (1.3cm). Make a series of connected straight stitches to form a stem for each cattail, then frame them with a leaf on either side. The stitch lengths vary from ¼" (6mm) to ½" (1.3cm). Slip the bottom stitches under the cygnet's tail.

5. Make sure your floss ends are neatly knotted and trimmed. Pull the fabric edges on all sides to tighten the center fabric a final time. Working on the back side of the hoop, cut the fabric edges so that a 1" (2.5cm) hem remains. Iron the hem so that it lies flat against the back of the hoop and extends behind the stitching, or stitch and gather the hem in place: Thread a sewing needle with a length of thread and make a running stitch ¼" (6mm) from the cut edge. Pull the beginning and end of the thread to gather the hem, then knot the ends together. Stitch a decorative fabric or felt circle over the back of the hoop to completely conceal your stitching. Tie a hanging ribbon to the top screw or balance the back of the hoop on a nail.

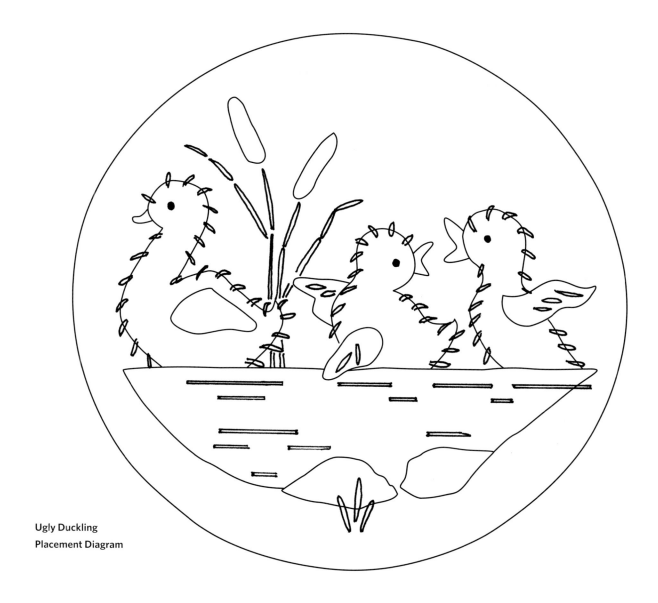

Ugly Duckling
Placement Diagram

Frog Prince Embroidery

THIS FROG IS CATCHING FLIES BY THE POND, just waiting for his princess to arrive.

Note: Use embroidery stitches to attach the felt pieces; no seam allowances are added.

Dimensions: 6" (15.2cm)

MATERIALS

Templates on page 113

6" (15.2cm) embroidery hoop

10" (25.4cm) square heavyweight muslin

Wool felt in moss green, lime green, turquoise, white and light-orange

Embroidery floss in white, mustard, green, light-yellow, light-blue and black

2 black glass eyes

Sewing thread (optional)

TOOLS

Scissors

Straight pins

Embroidery and sewing needles

Iron and ironing board

Sewing needle (optional)

1. Using the method described in the Ugly Duckling Embroidery, the templates and the placement diagram on the next page for reference, cut the following pattern pieces out of felt and layer them over the stretched muslin:

- From moss green felt, cut the frog back and back leg.
- From lime green felt, cut the frog body and front legs.
- From turquoise felt, cut both lilypads.
- From white felt, cut all 3 flower pieces.
- From light-orange felt, cut the crown.

2. Follow the method outlined in Step 4 of Ugly Duckling Embroidery and the placement diagram on the next page to complete the stitching:

Green: Make small stitches around the outside of the lime green frog body piece to hold it in place. Make slightly larger stitches around the frog legs and at each frog toe. Next, make a line of more visible stitches along the inside edge of the moss green back.

Black: Stitch a black glass bead eye into the forehead cavities in the front of the head. Create a wide grin with a series of 2 connected stitches.

White: Make dragonfly wings on either side of the frog's head with two ½" (1.3cm) cross-stitches.

Mustard: Embellish the moss green frog back with a pattern of *V*-shaped stitches, beginning and ending with a single *V* but increasing to 3 *V*'s per row for 4 rows.

Light-Yellow: Decorate each crown point with a lazy daisy stitch, then add a French knot over each crown tip. Make 3

vertical straight-stitch stamens in the center of each lily flower. Adjust the length of the stamens to the size of the flowers. Cap each stamen with a short horizontal straight stitch. Intersect the dragonfly wings with a ½" (1.3cm) straight stitch for the body.

Light-Blue: Refer to the diagram to position a series of straight, horizontal water lines. The stitches are shorter in the background and longer in the foreground.

3. Finish your project following Step 5 of Ugly Duckling Embroidery.

**Frog Prince
Placement Diagram**

Little Red Hen Embroidery

INSPIRED BY VINTAGE STITCHERY, this little red hen contentedly harvests wheat while her busy chicks trail behind.

Note: Use embroidery stitches to attach the felt pieces; no seam allowances are added.

Dimensions: 6" (15.2cm)

MATERIALS

Pattern pieces on page 114

6" (15.2cm) embroidery hoop

10" (25.4cm) square heavyweight muslin

Wool felt in lime green, light-orange, brown, light-yellow, light-blue and red

Embroidery floss in yellow, white, mustard, brown, orange, red and black

White sewing thread

TOOLS

Scissors

Straight pins

Embroidery and sewing needles

---

1. Using the method described in the Ugly Duckling Embroidery, the templates and the placement diagram on the next page for reference, cut the following pattern pieces out of felt and layer them over the stretched muslin:

- From lime green felt, cut the foreground and background.
- From light-orange felt, cut the hen body.
- From light-yellow felt, cut 2 chicks and the hen wing.
- From brown felt, cut the hen tail feather.
- From light-blue felt, cut the apron and bow.
- From red felt, cut the beak and comb.

2. Follow the method outlined in Step 4 of Ugly Duckling Embroidery and the placement diagram on the next page to complete the stitching:

Yellow: Stitch the wheat blades ½" to ¾" (1.3cm to 1.9cm), varying their orientation along the bottom edge of the lime green felt. Make 5 longer wheat stalks stems ¾" (1.9cm) to 1¼" (3.2cm) topped with a smaller ⅓" (8mm) to ¼" (6mm) stitch.

Mustard: Top each wheat stalk with a series of ⅛" (3mm) diagonal stitches. Whipstitch the outside edge of the hen's wing, and make two ¼" (6mm) straight stitches to tack down the indentations in the wing feathers. Make 3 straight stitches in the tail feather piece, from ⅛" (3mm) to ⅓" (8mm). Give each chick a V-shaped wing stitch. Make two ¼" (6mm) vertical stitches for the legs on each chick. End each leg with a ¼" (6mm) horizontal stitch for the feet.

Black: Make a French knot eye in the center of the chicks' heads. Make an ⅛" (3mm) *V*-stitch for the hen's eye. Add 2 more straight stitches for eyelashes. Make a straight stitch that intersects the center of the hen's beak.

White: Make 4 rows of straight stitches down the hen's neck. Start at the top with ⅛" (3mm) stitches and increase the stitches in length to ¼" (6mm) in the final row. Make 6 V-stitch feathers on the hen's tail. Refer to the diagram for stitch orientation; the last 2 stitches are parallel to the tail edge.

Red: Using a single strand of floss and tiny stitches, tack down the comb and beak. Using 3 strands of floss, whipstitch around the bottom edge of the apron. Make two ¼" (6mm)

straight stitches through the center of the bow, anchoring it and the apron in place.

Orange: Make an ⅛" (3mm) V-stitch for each chick's beak. The open end of the first chick's beak faces out; the second chick's beak is reversed.

Brown: Make the hen's legs with 2 side-by-side ½" (1.3cm) stitches. The stitches extend from the base of the felt and end at the center of the foot. Make 4 straight stitches for each chicken foot: the back claw is ¼" (6mm) and the 3 front claws are ⅓" (8mm), radiating out at a slight angle. Create a worm in the chick's closed beak. Use 4 to 5 connected stitches about ⅛" (3mm) to ¼" (6mm) long to make an *n* shape.

3. Finish your project following Step 5 of Ugly Duckling Embroidery.

**LIttle Red Hen
Placement Diagram**

Cinderella's Shoes

WHEN OUR DAUGHTER WAS A TODDLER, I quickly realized that a passion for shoes can begin at a young age. Unlike real shoes, these unique pillows won't be outgrown after a single season. Glass slippers aren't always practical for today's "can-do" girls; add walking or cowboy boots to the throw pillow arrangement. Have fun mixing and matching fabrics from your stash, and be sure to incorporate leftover trim and odd buttons.

All the pillows are assembled the same way—just the pattern pieces, fabric colors and trims change.

Note: Do not add seam allowances; ¼" (6mm) seam allowances are included on the templates as needed.

Slipper Dimensions: 12" × 8" × 4" (30.5cm × 20.3cm × 10.2cm)

SLIPPER MATERIALS

Templates on page 115

¼ yard (0.2m) floral printed cotton

¼ yard (0.2m) turquoise cotton

Scrap of red plaid cotton

Wool felt in red

¼" (6mm) pink bias tape

½" (1.3cm) ivory lace

1" (2.5cm) blue shank button

Fiberfill stuffing

Sewing thread in coordinating colors

SLIPPER TOOLS

Sewing machine

Iron and ironing board

Scissors

Sewing needles

Straight pins

Slipper

1. Using the templates, cut out the following pattern pieces (do not add seam allowances, they are included where needed):

- From turquoise cotton, cut 2 pumps (flip template and cut 1 in reverse).
- From floral cotton, cut 2 pump sides (cut 1 in reverse).
- From red felt, cut 2 pump soles.
- From plaid scrap, cut 2 pump straps.

2. Stack and pin the plaid strap pieces right-sides together. Machine-stitch around the outside edge, leaving the flat bottom edge unsewn. Clip the curves in the seam allowance being careful not to clip into the stitching. Turn the strap right-side out and press it flat. Topstitch around the seamed edge.

3. With right sides facing up, lay a floral shoe side over each turquoise shoe. Align the bottom edges, then pin the top edge of the shoe side to the shoe piece under it. Slip the open strap end between the layers on 1 shoe side; refer to the template for exact placement. Stitch along the top edge of both shoe sides, catching the strap end in 1 of the seams (Figure 1).

4. Pin the bias tape over the sewn edge of both shoe sides and topstitch it in place. Pin the lace in place along the bias tape. Using a needle and thread, tack the lace in place with small hand-stitches.

5. Place a felt sole over each shoe, align the bottom edges and pin it in place. Topstitch ¼" (6mm) below the top edge (Figure 2).

6. Placing right sides together, pin the 2 shoes together. Align the trims and felt sole pieces at the toe and heel. Push the strap down between the layers so it stays away from the outside edge. Stitch around the outside edge, leaving a 2½" (6.4cm) opening in the middle back of the heel (Figure 3). Clip the curves in the seam allowance, being careful not to clip into the stitching, then turn the shoe right-side out.

7. Feed stuffing in through the opening and push it clear over to the toe. Firmly fill the toe, then stuff the arch and the high heel. Tuck the fabric and felt opening in and use red thread to hand-stitch the felt sides together.

8. Stretch the strap over to the other side of the toe and anchor it in place with the button. Sew the button shank through the strap and shoe, making several stitches to strengthen the connection.

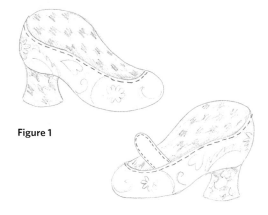

Figure 1

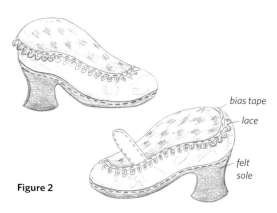

bias tape

lace

felt sole

Figure 2

right sides together

leave open

Figure 3

Cowboy Boot Dimensions: 18" × 10" × 5" (45.7cm × 25.4cm × 12.7cm)

Templates on page 116

¼ yard (0.2m) bird printed cotton

¼ yard (0.2m) mini-dot printed cotton

Scrap of green floral cotton

Wool felt in beige and red

¾" (1.9cm) brown rickrack

¼" (6mm) yellow bias tape

Two 1" (2.5cm) star buttons

Two ¾" (1.9cm) star buttons

Fiberfill stuffing

Sewing thread in coordinating colors

COWBOY BOOT TOOLS

Sewing maching

Iron and ironing board

Scissors

Sewing needles

Straight pins

Cowboy Boot

1. Using the templates, cut out the following pattern pieces (do not add seam allowances; they are included where needed):

- From the mini-dot cotton, cut 2 cowboy boots (flip the template and cut 1 in reverse).
- From the bird print cotton, cut 2 centers (cut 1 in reverse).
- From the green floral cotton scrap, cut 2 tops (cut 1 in reverse).
- From the beige felt, cut 2 bottom sections.
- From the red felt, cut 2 soles.

2. Like the slipper, first layer the fabrics to make 2 boot sides, stitch the pieces in place, then conceal the raw edges with bias tape (top join), and bottom felt piece and rickrack (bottom join). Sew the 2 sides together, leaving an opening in the back of the heel. Turn the boot right-side out, stuff and then sew the opening closed. Sew 2 star buttons (1 of each size) to each side.

Templates on page 115

¼ yard (0.2m) brown printed cotton

¼ yard (0.2m) red chevron printed
   cotton

¼ yard (0.2m) pink floral printed cotton

Wool felt in brown

Aqua pompom trim

¼" (6mm) pink bias tape

Fiberfill stuffing

Sewing thread in coordinating colors

WALKING BOOT TOOLS

Sewing machine

Iron and ironing board

Scissors

Sewing needles

Straight pins

Walking Boot Dimensions: 15" × 10" × 5" (38.1cm × 25.4cm × 12.7cm)

Walking Boot

1. Using the templates, cut out the following pattern pieces (do not add seam allowances, they are included where needed):

- From brown printed cotton, cut 2 walking boots (flip the template and cut 1 in reverse).
- From pink floral printed cotton, cut 2 boot fronts (cut 1 in reverse).
- From red chevron printed cotton, cut 2 boot sides (cut 1 in reverse).
- From brown felt, cut 2 boot soles.

2. Like the cowboy boot, create the boot sides by layering. Position the boot shaft pieces (front over center) vertically on the walking boot pieces. Stitch the pieces in place and then conceal the raw edges where the different fabrics meet with pompom trim down the shaft and bias tape across the ankle. Sew the 2 sides together, leaving an opening in the brown felt heel. Turn the boot right-side out, stuff and then sew the opening closed.

Dragon

A FAR CRY FROM THE THRASHING, FIRE-BREATHING DRAGONS OF KNIGHTLY TALES, this soft and sweet fellow will have a starring role in your child's bedtime routine. Layers of plush fur and flannel are stitched and stuffed to create the perfect, huggable friend. He's not a complete wimp, though; his wide base allows him to stand upright and defend block castles and pillow forts from daytime attacks.

Note: Pattern pieces include a ¼" (6mm) seam allowance.

Dimensions: 18" × 14½" × 16" (45.7cm × 36.8cm × 40.6cm)

MATERIALS

Templates on page 117

1 yard (0.9m) green polyester chenille fabric

½ yard (0.5m) white polyester chenille fabric

¼ yard (0.2m) turquoise flannel

6" (15.2cm) square of red flannel

⅝" (1.6cm) yellow and black safety eyes

Fiberfill stuffing

Sewing thread in coordinating colors

TOOLS

Sewing machine

Scissors

Embroidery and sewing needles

Straight pins

Stuffing stick

1. Using the templates, cut out the following pattern pieces (do not add seam allowances; they are included):

- From the green chenille, cut 2 bodies (flip template and cut 1 in reverse), 2 wings (1 in reverse), 2 ears (1 in reverse), 4 arms (2 in reverse), 4 green thigh/foot top pieces (2 in reverse) and 1 head insert.
- From the white chenille, cut 2 ears (1 in reverse) and 1 belly insert.
- From the turquoise flannel, cut 2 wings (1 in reverse) and 2 feet bottoms.
- From the red flannel, cut 2 tongue pieces.

2. Stack and pin the 2 pairs of arms right sides together. Stitch around the outside edge to join the 2 layers, leaving the shoulder end open. Turn the arms right-side out and stuff.

3. Placing right sides together, pair a green ear piece with each white ear piece. Machine-stitch around the outside edge, leaving the bottom edge open. Trim the selvedge off the tips, then turn the ears right-side out. Smooth them flat with your fingers, then topstitch around the outside edge (Figure 1). Fold the base of the ears in half, trapping the white on the inside. Machine-stitch across the folded base to secure the shaping (Figure 2).

4. Placing right sides together, stack a flannel wing over each green wing, making sure you have a left and right wing. Pin and then machine-stitch along the outside edge. Leave the flat end of the wing unstitched. Turn the wings right-side out and smooth them flat. Topstitch around the outside edge (Figure 3).

5. To shape the wings, stitch the marked fold lines on the pattern: Fold the fabric along the line, flannel on the inside, and make a straight seam through all 4 fabric layers, ¼" (6mm) from the folded edge. Repeat to create the second fold line in the first wing (Figure 4). Repeat the process to make 2 more fold lines in the second wing. Fold the open end of each wing in half, flannel on the inside, then machine-stitch the fold to secure the shaping (Figure 5).

6. Pin the tongue pieces right sides together. Machine-stitch around the outside edge, leaving the flat end open. Trim the points, then use a stuffing stick to turn the tongue right-side out. Iron the tongue flat then topstitch around the outside edge (Figure 6a). Center the finished tongue between the flat ends of the head and belly insert pieces (Figure 6b). Place right sides together and then seam through all 3 pieces.

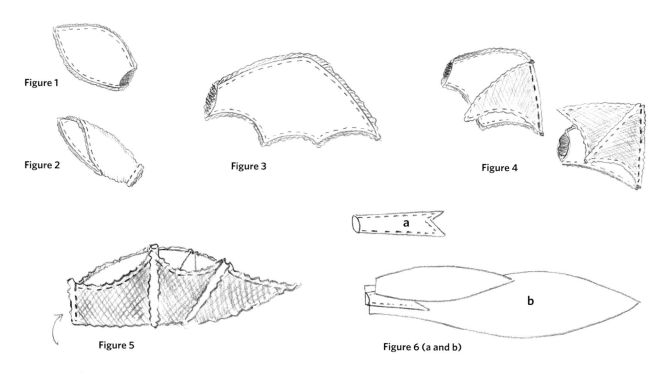

Figure 1

Figure 2

Figure 3

Figure 4

Figure 5

Figure 6 (a and b)

7. Assemble and stitch the body pieces and inserts together. Pin the body pieces together positioning the connected belly and head inserts, arms, ears and wings between them. Refer to the templates for exact positioning. Be sure that all right sides are together. Arms, tongue, ears and wings should all be hidden inside, with just their ends extending between the edges of the insert and body fabric (Figure 7).

Pin around both sides of the insert, pinning the body pieces together where the insert ends. Machine-stitch around the dragon, leaving a 3" (7.6cm) opening under the wings to turn the dragon right-side out. Check that you caught all the pieces in your seam, then turn the dragon right-side out.

8. Refer to the template for positioning, then snip a small opening on either side of the head. Insert the screw end of each safety eye into a hole. Slide the plastic backing piece up the screw end until it rests snugly against the wrong side of the green fabric. Fill the head and tail with stuffing first, then continue to fill the rest of the body cavity. The fabric has a lot of stretch, so be careful not to overstuff and distort your creation.

9. Placing right sides together, pin the thigh/foot top pieces together. Machine-stitch them together, leaving both the base of the foot and the ankle/heel portion unstitched. Don't remove the pins from the ankle/heel portion; leave them in place so that the top of the foot fits properly over the foot piece (Figure 8a). Center the connected foot top over the flannel foot piece, line up the toes and heel, and pin them in place (Figure 8b). Machine-stitch around the outside edge of the foot. Turn the feet right-side out through the ankle opening. Stuff the toes first, then fill the thigh. Hand-stitch the opening closed (Figure 8c). Repeat the process to complete the second foot. Refer to the body template for placement, then hand-stitch a finished thigh/foot top to each side of the body.

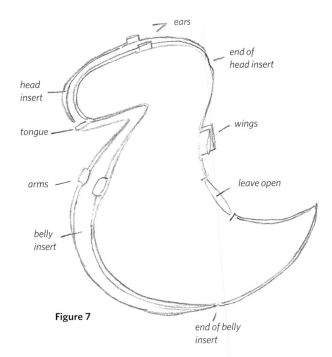

Figure 7

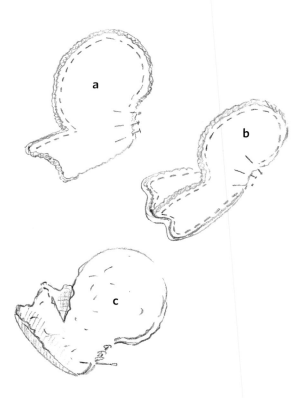

Figure 8 (a, b and c)

Medieval Castle

A BUILDER'S DREAM: four walls, a floor and a drawbridge hook together to make a full-blown castle in seconds. It's an instant play space for plastic toys and ideal for travel to faraway lands, like Grandma's house. Posterboard sections slide between the fabric walls to give them substance.

 Note: Add ¼" (6mm) seam allowances to the indicated pattern pieces only.

Dimensions: 11" × 12" × 9" (27.9cm × 30.5cm × 22.9cm)

MATERIALS

Templates on page 116

½ yard (0.5m) white printed cotton

½ yard (0.5m) white flag printed cotton

½ yard (0.5m) bright printed cotton

1 yard (0.9m) fusible fleece interfacing

2 sheets of posterboard

Wool felt in brown and black

24" (61cm) blue hook-and-loop fastener, cut in 6" (15.2cm) pieces

16½" (41.9cm) green hook-and-loop fastener, cut in 2¾" (7cm) pieces

3" (7.6cm) red hook-and-loop fastener

Sewing thread in coordinating colors

TOOLS

Iron and ironing board

Scissors (paper and fabric)

Sewing machine

Straight pins

Stuffing stick

---

1. Using the templates, cut out the following pattern pieces, adding a ¼" (6mm) seam allowance:

- From the white printed cotton, cut a castle front and back.
- From the white flag printed cotton, cut 2 castle sides and 1 castle door.
- From the bright printed cotton, cut 1 castle front, 1 castle back and 2 castle sides.
- From the brown felt, cut 1 castle door and a 12" × 9⅛" (30.5cm × 23.3cm) rectangle for the castle floor.

- From the black felt, cut 1 castle floor with the same dimensions as the brown felt piece.
- From the fusible fleece lining, cut the following pieces with no seam allowance: 1 castle front, 1 castle back, 2 castle sides and 1 castle door.
- From the posterboard, cut the following lining pieces ¼" (6mm) smaller than the pattern pieces: 1 castle front, 1 castle back, 2 castle sides, 1 castle door and 1 castle floor.

2. Iron a fleece lining piece to each outer castle piece: white printed cotton castle front and back, 2 flag printed cotton castle sides and 1 castle door.

3. Center the loop portion of the red hook-and-loop fastener above the door on the bright printed cotton castle front piece and stitch it in place (Figure 1).

4. Placing right sides together, pin each white printed castle piece with its colorful, bright printed counterpart and pin.

5. Insert blue hook-and-loop fastener between each front and back pairing, 2" (5.1cm) from the bottom edge. Insert the hook sections into the front and back walls and the loop sections into the side walls. Line up the length of the outside fastener edge with the fabric edges.

6. Machine-stitch the fabric pairs together, trapping the hook-and-loop fastener in your seams. Sew up 1 side, across the top and back down the other side, leaving the bottom edge unsewn (Figure 2). Do not stitch the door portion of the castle front. Trim away the excess fabric from the corners.

7. Turn the finished pieces right-side out. Use a stuffing stick to push out the corners so that the top edges are square. Insert the corresponding posterboard piece into each wall, carefully feeding the turrets into position first (Figure 3). Try not to bend the board; a crease will weaken it.

8. Tuck the fabric edges under, and using just the hook portion of the green hook-and-loop fastener, center sections on either side of the front wall, center a single section on each side wall, and position 2 sections on the back wall 1½" (3.8cm) from the outside edge. Orient all the fastener pieces so that the flat side faces front and the hook portion faces the inner, brightly colored side.

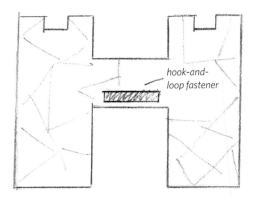

hook-and-loop fastener

Figure 1

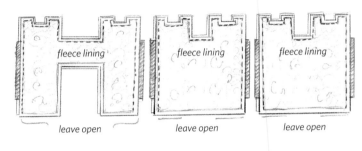

fleece lining   *fleece lining*   *fleece lining*

leave open   *leave open*   *leave open*

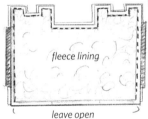

fleece lining

Figure 2

leave open

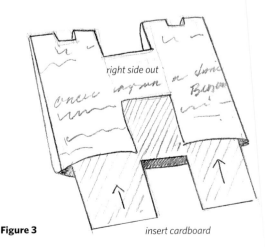

right side out

Figure 3   *insert cardboard*

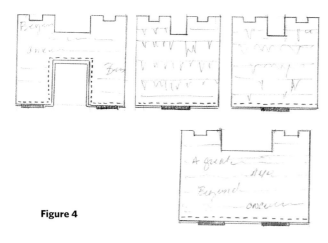

Figure 4

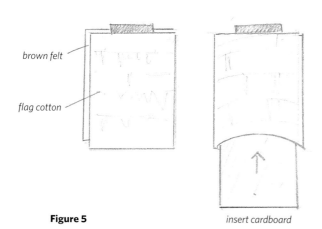

brown felt

flag cotton

Figure 5

insert cardboard

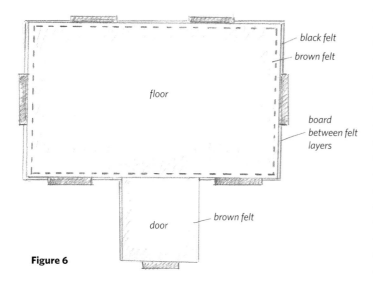

black felt

brown felt

floor

board between felt layers

door

brown felt

Figure 6

9. Iron the tucked fabric edges around the door opening on the front wall piece. Make sure the front and back fabric edges line up. Manipulate the posterboard between the fabric layers; push it to the top and outside, giving yourself room to stitch across the bottom edges and around the door. Starting at the outside corner of the wall, begin stitching across the base, trapping the fastener. Turn around the corners to frame the outside edge of the door, and then finish by seaming across the other base section.

10. Manipulate the posterboard through the fabric layers of the back wall piece so it's pushed up against the top of the wall. Align the bottom edge of the wall under your presser foot and machine-stitch from 1 side to the other. Be sure you're only stitching through the top and bottom fabric layers and the fastener in between (Figure 4). Repeat the process with the remaining 2 side walls.

11. Placing right sides together, pin the white fabric door to the brown door. Insert the remaining red hook section of the fastener between the layers. The hook side should face the white fabric. Stitch around the outside side and top edges, catching the fastener in your seam. Leave the bottom open. Trim the corners and turn the door right-side out. Insert the posterboard liner (Figure 5).

12. Assemble the castle floor: Sandwich the posterboard between the brown and black floor pieces, with the brown floor up. Insert the green loop sections on all 4 sides of the base piece: Center sections on the front corners, center a single section on each side, and position 2 on the back 1½" (3.8cm) from each outside edge. Orient all the fastener pieces so that the loop side faces up. Center the door on the front side, brown side up, inserting the unsewn edge between the layers. Use the finished walls to double check the door and fastener positioning. Stitch around all 4 sides, catching the fastener and door in your seam.

Stone Soup Pot and Veggies

PULL OUT YOUR FABRIC STASH and stitch a bountiful pot of vegetables, enough to satisfy even the hungriest soldier. Most of these veggies use only two to three pieces of fabric and are quickly trimmed with felt leaves. The fabric-lined felt pot does double duty; it's perfect for mixing your child's original recipes and storing the vegetables when it's time to clean up.

Note: Add ¼" (6mm) seam allowances to the indicated pattern pieces only.

Pot Dimensions: 6¼" × 9" (15.9cm × 22.9cm)

MATERIALS

Templates on page 118

¼ yard (0.2m) each of black, gray, yellow-green, tan and green wool felt

¼ yard (0.2m) aqua diamond printed cotton

¼ yard (0.2m) olive green printed cotton (cabbage)

¼ yard (0.2m) purple printed cotton (eggplant)

¼ yard (0.2m) orange printed cotton (carrot)

¼ yard (0.2m) red printed cotton (tomato)

¼ yard (0.2m) yellow-green printed cotton (celery)

¼ yard (0.2m) tan printed cotton (potato)

¼ yard (0.2m) white printed cotton (garlic)

Sewing thread in coordinating colors

Fiberfill stuffing

TOOLS

Scissors

Sewing machine

Sewing needles

Straight pins

Stuffing stick

Pot Instructions

1. Using the templates, cut the following pattern pieces adding a ¼" (6mm) seam allowance as indicated:

- From black felt, cut 1 pot base (add seam allowance) and 4 pot handles.
- From gray felt, cut a 25¼" × 6¾" (64.1cm × 17.1cm) rectangle.
- From the aqua diamond printed cotton, cut 1 pot side (dimensions above) and 1 pot base (add seam allowance).

2. Pin the bottom edge of the gray felt rectangle around the outside edge of the black base piece. Machine-stitch a continuous seam around the base piece to connect the 2 pieces together (Figure 1).

3. Pin the ends of the gray side piece together. Make a vertical seam to connect the pinned ends.

4. Repeat steps 2 and 3 with the cotton pot pieces.

5. Placing right sides together, insert the lining into the pot (Figure 2). Line up the edges and pin them together. Make a continuous seam through both layers around the top of the pot. Leave a 3" (7.6cm) opening between the beginning and end of the seam (Figure 3).

6. Pull the pot right-side out through the opening and smooth the lining inside the pot. Tuck in the fabric edges of the opening. Topstitch around the pot edge, ¼" (6mm) from the top seamed edge. If necessary, hand-stitch the opening closed with small stitches to match the machine-stitching.

7. Pin 2 felt handles together. Use black thread and machine-stitch around the outside edge. Repeat with the second handle.

8. Pin the handles to either side of the pot so that the rounded base portion is 1¼" (3.2cm) from the top edge. Use black thread and hand-stitch the base portion of the handle to the gray felt side. The top of the handle should extend above the pot edge (Figure 4).

Potato (makes 1)

1. Using the templates, cut the following pattern pieces, adding a ¼" (6mm) seam allowance:

- From tan printed cotton, cut 1 potato.
- From tan felt, cut 1 potato.

2. Placing right sides together, pin and stitch the fabric potato side to the felt potato side. Machine-stitch around the outside edge leaving a 1½" (3.8cm) opening to turn the potato (Figure 5).

3. Turn the potato right-side out. Stuff the rounded bumpy edges first, then stuff completely. Tuck in the fabric edges and use small invisible stitches to close the opening.

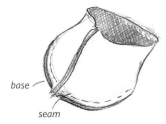

base

seam

Figure 1

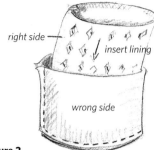

right side

insert lining

wrong side

Figure 2

leave open

seam around top

Figure 3

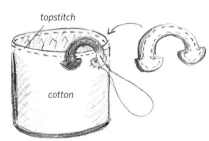

topstitch

cotton

Figure 4

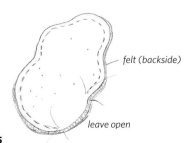

felt (backside)

leave open

Figure 5

Eggplant

1. Using the templates, cut the following pattern pieces, adding a ¼" (6mm) seam allowance:

- From purple printed cotton, cut 3 eggplant sides.
- From tan felt, cut 3 eggplant tops.

2. Placing right sides together, pin the cotton sides together. Make 3 separate seams to connect the sides: 2 seams extending from bottom to top, and the third seam ending a couple of inches (centimeters) before the top, leaving an opening to turn the eggplant right-side out.

3. Turn the eggplant right-side out, stuff and hand-stitch the opening closed.

4. Placing right sides together, pin and stitch the sides and tops of the 3 tops together. Leave the pointed leaf portion of the leaves unsewn. Turn the sewn piece right-side out.

5. Insert a pinch of stuffing into the stem portion of the top. Place the stuffed top over the small end of the eggplant. Line up a pointed leaf end in the center of each eggplant side (Figure 6). Hand-stitch the bottom edge to the eggplant with small invisible stitches.

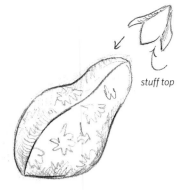

stuff top

Figure 6

Carrot (makes 1)

1. Using the templates, cut the following pattern pieces, adding a ¼" (6mm) seam allowance where indicated:

- From orange printed cotton, cut 3 carrot sides (add seam allowance).
- From green felt, cut 2 carrot tops.

2. Placing right sides together, pin the 3 carrot sides together. Make 3 separate seams to connect the sides, starting each seam ½" (1.3cm) from the top edge and ending at the base (Figure 7).

3. Pull the carrot right-side out through the opening. Push the stuffing into the base first, using a stuffing stick. Continue stuffing the rest of the carrot.

4. Pair the carrot tops together and make a single seam up the center of the carrot top from the base to ½" (1.3cm) from the top.

5. Fold the seamed tops open and push the ends down into the opening in the carrot top. Tuck in the fabric edges on either side of the carrot tops. Hand-stitch from 1 side of the tucked edges through the base of the carrot tops to the other side of the fabric. Sew back and forth, closing the carrot while anchoring the tops in place (Figure 8).

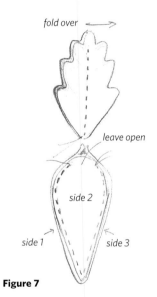

fold over

leave open

side 2

side 1   side 3

Figure 7

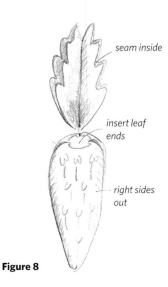

seam inside

insert leaf ends

right sides out

Figure 8

Figure 9

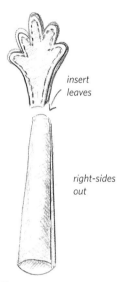

insert leaves

right-sides out

Figure 10

attach top

stuff here

Figure 11

Celery (makes 1)

1. Using the templates, cut the following pattern pieces, adding a ¼" (6mm) seam allowance where indicated:

- From yellow-green printed cotton, cut 2 celery stalks (add seam allowance).
- From yellow-green felt, cut 1 celery base and 2 celery tops.

2. Placing right sides together, pin the base of each stalk to 1 side of the felt base piece. Make a separate seam on either side of the base piece to connect the stalks to the base.

3. Keeping the right sides together, pin then stitch up either side of the fabric stalks. Leave the top edge open (Figure 9). Pull the finished stalk right-side out through the opening.

4. Stack, pin and stitch the felt celery tops together. Machine-stitch a continuous ¼" (6mm) seam from the outside leaf edge.

5. Stuff the base of the stalk first, then fill the length of the stalk with a stuffing stick. Push the base of the tops down into the stalk opening, tuck in the fabric edges and hand-stitch the opening closed (Figure 10). Be sure to catch the base of the felt tops in each stitch.

Tomato

1. Using the templates, cut the following pattern pieces, adding a ¼" (6mm) seam allowance where indicated:

- From red printed cotton, cut 6 tomato sides (add seam allowance).
- From green felt, cut 1 tomato top.

2. Placing right sides together, pin the 6 tomato sides together. Make 6 separate seams to connect them: 5 seams spanning from top to bottom, and the sixth seam with a 2" (5.1cm) opening at the base.

3. Turn the tomato right-side out and generously fill it, being careful not to overstuff or distort its shape. Tuck in the fabric edges and use small invisible stitches to sew the opening closed.

4. Lay the top over the side with the hand-stitched closure. Make small stitches through the center of the top, leaving the pointed ends unattached (Figure 11).

Cabbage

1. Using the templates, cut the following pattern pieces adding a ¼" (6mm) seam allowance:

- From dark green printed cotton, cut 4 cabbage sides.
- From the green felt, cut 4 cabbage leaves.

2. Placing right sides together, pin together the cotton sides and felt leaves. Sandwich the straight edge of a felt leaf piece between the cotton side pieces. The bumpy felt leaf edges should extend freely into the center.

3. Make 4 separate seams to attach the cabbage sides together. Three of the seams should start at the top and end at the base. The fourth seam should stop a few inches (centimeters) before the base, to allow an opening to turn the cabbage right-side out (Figure 12).

4. Turn the cabbage right-side out, stuff and hand-stitch the opening closed.

Garlic

1. Using the template, cut 10 garlic sides from the white printed cotton, adding a ¼" (6mm) seam allowance.

2. Placing right sides together, pin and stitch the flat sides of the 10 pieces first. Pair 5 sets of garlic sides and make 5 separate seams to stitch the flat side of each pair together (Figure 13a).

3. Keeping right sides together, pin and stitch the rounded sides. Make 5 separate seams from top to bottom to connect the rounded sides. Stop the last seam 1" (2.5cm) before the base (Figure 13b).

4. Pull the garlic right-side out through the bottom opening. Smooth a rounded side flat and make a 1" (2.5cm) seam from the top of the garlic; position the seam ¼" (6mm) from the seamed edge. Repeat the process with the 4 remaining rounded sides (Figure 13c).

5. Push stuffing up through the opening in the base. Fill each of the rounded sides but leave the flat connections between them concave. Tuck in the fabric edges and make small invisible stitches to close the opening.

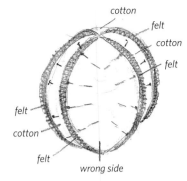

cotton
felt
cotton
felt
felt
cotton
felt
wrong side

Figure 12

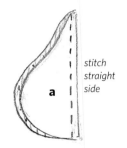

stitch straight side

a

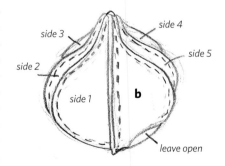

side 3
side 4
side 2
side 5
side 1
b
leave open

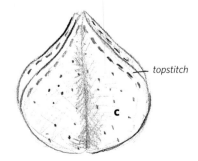

topstitch
c

Figure 13 (a, b and c)

Rapunzel Pillow

THIS SOFT AND CUDDLY PILLOW brings the classic bedtime fairy tale to life. Rapunzel comes out of her pocket to reenact her famous story and cuddle with your child. When returned to her pillow, Rapunzel searches for princes from atop her castle tower. Quick and simple to sew, three pieces of fabric are joined together in a single seam to form the front of the pillow.

 Note: Add ¼" (6mm) seam allowances to the indicated pattern pieces only.

Dimensions: Pillow 12" × 16" (30.5cm × 40.6cm); Doll 7" × 4" (17.8cm × 10.2cm)

MATERIALS

Pillow

¼ yard (0.2m) stone printed cotton

½ yard (0.5m) gray chevron printed cotton

½ yard (0.2m) blue sky printed cotton

½ yard (0.2m) white plush polyester fabric

12" × 16" (30.5cm × 40.6cm) down pillow form

Sewing thread in coordinating colors

Rapunzel Doll

Templates on page 119

Scrap of floral printed cotton

Wool felt in orange, red, gold, blue and skin tone

Fiberfill stuffing

Embroidery floss in gold, red and black

TOOLS

Sewing machine

Iron and ironing board

Rotary cutter

Cutting mat

Ruler

Scissors

Embroidery and sewing needles

Straight pins

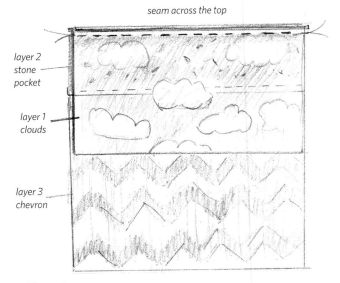

Pillow

1. Cut the following pieces with a rotary cutter, ruler and cutting mat:

- From the chevron printed cotton, cut an 8½" × 13" (21.6cm × 33cm) rectangle.
- From the stone printed cotton, cut a 9" × 13" (22.9cm × 33cm) rectangle.
- From the blue sky printed cotton, cut a 9" × 13" (22.9cm × 33cm) rectangle.
- From the white plush fabric, cut a 12½" × 16½" (31.8cm × 41.9cm) rectangle.

2. Fold the stone fabric in half lengthwise, right sides out, so it measures 4½" × 13" (11.4cm × 33cm). Press the folded fabric flat. Topstitch a straight seam ¼" (6mm) from the pressed fold (Figure 1).

3. With right sides together, place the sky piece over the chevron piece. Insert the stone fabric pocket, seam side down, between the layers. Line up all 4 cut edges together. Make a single seam across the top (Figure 2). Press the seam flat, and fold the pocket up to lay it over the sky.

4. Placing right sides together, lay the plush fabric back over the pillow front, and pin the edges together. Machine-stitch around the outside edge, leaving a 5" (12.7cm) opening (Figure 3). Check your seams, trim the corners and turn the pillow right-side out through the opening.

5. Compress the pillow form to squeeze it into the opening. Make sure the pillow corners fill the pillowcase corners. Tuck in the fabric edges at the opening and hand-stitch them closed.

topstitch along fold

Figure 1

seam across the top

layer 2 stone pocket

layer 1 clouds

layer 3 chevron

Figure 2

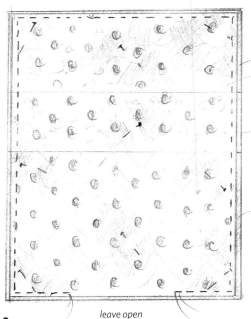

backside

leave open

Figure 3

Rapunzel Doll

1. Using the templates, cut the following pattern pieces, adding a ¼" (6mm) seam allowance where indicated:

- From the floral printed cotton, cut 2 body pieces (add seam allowance).
- From the red felt, cut 1 arm piece.
- From the orange felt, cut the hood front and hood back.
- From the skin tone felt, cut 2 hands and 1 face.
- From the gold felt, cut Rapunzel's hair and three 1" × 13" (2.5cm × 33cm) strips.
- From the blue felt, cut a ½" × 3½" (1.3cm × 8.9cm) strip.

2. Arrange the front felt pieces over the cotton body and machine-stitch them in place ⅛" (3mm) from the raw edges: Place the arms over the center of the body, then tuck a hand under each sleeve. Lay the front hood over the top of the arms. Center the face and bangs in the hood. Use white thread to stitch the face, hands, bangs and base of the hood. Switch to red thread to stitch the arms.

3. Embroider Rapunzel's face: Use 3 strands of red floss and make a ¼" (6mm) *V*-stitch to form the mouth. Use 3 strands of black floss to make the eyes: Each eye is an ⅛" (3mm) inverted *V*-stitch framed by an ⅛" (3mm) diagonal lash. Make a gold ¼" (6mm) slanted eyebrow over each eye using 3 strands of floss (Figure 4).

4. Fold the top of each of the 3 hair strips in half to make them ½" (1.3cm) wide. Stack them together and machine-stitch across the top to hold them together. Braid the length, folding the strips as you work your way down. Stop ½" (1.3cm) before you reach the end of the strips. Machine-stitch the ends together. Tie the blue strip around the braid, covering the stitched ends.

5. Lay the hood back over the top of the second cotton body. Tuck the top of the braid off center under the hood. Use white thread to stitch along the bottom edge of the hood, trapping the braid in the seam between the hood and the cotton body (Figure 5).

6. Pin the front of the body to the back of the body, right sides together. Fold the braid in half and tuck it between the layers so it doesn't get caught in the seaming. Machine-stitch around the outside edge, leaving a 1½" (3.8cm) opening at the base of the cotton fabric.

7. Turn the doll right-side out through the opening. Stuff her, filling the head first and then the rest of the body. Don't overstuff; she should remain flat to fit in the castle pillow pocket. Tuck in the cut fabric edges and hand-stitch the opening closed.

Figure 4

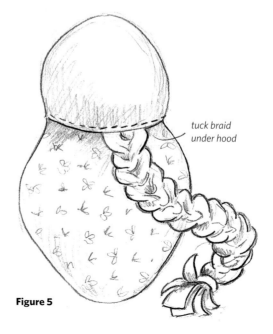

tuck braid under hood

Figure 5

Jack and the Beanstalk Pillow

A VARIATION ON THE RAPUNZEL PILLOW, this pillow features fearless Jack, climbing his way to the top of the beanstalk. Jack's castle in the beanstalk is made by joining the sky and beanstalk fabrics vertically, then layering two sets of chevron fabric rectangles to create a pocket in the upper right corner.

Note: Add ¼" (6mm) seam allowances to the indicated pattern pieces only.

Dimensions: Pillow 12" × 16" (30.5cm × 40.6cm); Doll 7" × 4" (17.8cm × 10.2cm)

MATERIALS

Pillow

¼ yard (0.2m) green leaves printed cotton

¼ yard (0.2m) gray chevron printed cotton

¼ yard (0.2m) gray mini-chevron printed cotton

¼ yard (0.2m) blue sky printed cotton

½ yard (0.5m) white plush polyester fabric

12" × 16" (30.5cm × 40.6cm) down pillow form

Sewing thread in coordinating colors

Jack Doll

Templates on page 119

Scrap of brown printed cotton

Wool felt in black, olive green, brown, red and skin tone

Fiberfill stuffing

Embroidery floss in brown, red and black

TOOLS

Sewing machine

Iron and ironing board

Rotary cutter

Cutting mat

Ruler

Scissors

Embroidery and sewing needles

Straight pins

Pillow

1. Cut the following pieces with a rotary cutter, ruler and cutting mat:

- From the blue sky printed cotton, cut a 4½" × 16½" (11.4cm × 41.9cm) rectangle.
- From the green leaves printed cotton, cut an 8¾" × 16½" (22.2cm × 41.9cm) rectangle.
- From the gray chevron printed cotton, cut two 6" × 9½" (15.2cm × 24.1cm) rectangles.
- From the gray mini-chevron, cut two 5¼" × 6" (13.3cm × 15.2cm) rectangles.
- From the white plush fabric, cut a 12½" × 16½" (31.8cm × 41.9cm) rectangle.

2. Pair and pin the large chevron rectangles, right sides together. Machine-stitch down 1 side and across the bottom, leaving the top and other side open (Figure 1a). Trim the corner, turn right-side out and press flat. Pair and pin the smaller mini-chevron rectangles right sides together. Machine-stitch the top, side and bottom edges together, leaving the other side open (Figure 1b). Trim the corners and turn the piece right-side out; press flat.

3. Placing right sides together, pair the sky piece with the green leaves piece. Make a single vertical seam to join them together (Figure 2). Press the seam flat.

4. Pin the large chevron pocket over the upper right corner, matching the unsewn edges with the top and side edges of the pillow front. Pin the smaller mini-chevron pocket over the bottom of the large chevron pocket. Line up the finished side and bottom edges of both chevron pieces; the unsewn edges should line up with the pillow edge (Figure 3). Make a single seam down the finished side edge of the pockets, turn at the corner and seam across the bottom. The top and side edges will be sewn when you attach the pillow back.

5. Placing right sides together, lay the plush fabric back over the pillow front, and pin the edges together. Machine-stitch around the outside edge, leaving a 5" (12.7cm) opening. Check your seams, trim the corners and turn the pillow right-side out through the opening.

6. Compress the pillow form to squeeze it into the opening. Make sure the pillow corners fill the pillowcase corners. Tuck in the fabric edges at the opening and hand-stitch them closed.

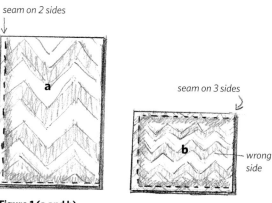

seam on 2 sides

seam on 3 sides

wrong side

Figure 1 (a and b)

seam sky to green leaves

right sides together

Figure 2

seam to pillow front

Figure 3

Jack Doll

1. Using the templates, cut the following pattern pieces, adding a ¼" (6mm) seam allowance where indicated:

- From the brown printed cotton, cut 2 body pieces (add seam allowance).
- From the brown felt, cut 1 arm piece and 1 hair piece.
- From the black felt, cut 1 hood front and 1 hood back piece.
- From the skin tone felt, cut 2 hands and 1 face.
- From the olive green felt, cut 2 hat pieces.
- From the red felt, cut 1 feather.

2. Arrange the front felt pieces over the cotton body: Place the arms over the center of the body, then tuck a hand under each sleeve. Lay the hood over the top of the arms. Center the face and bangs on the hood. Stitch the pieces in place using white thread for the face and hands, brown thread for the bangs and arms, and black thread for the base of the hood.

3. Embroider Jack's face using 3 strands of red floss to make a ⅜" (10mm) V-stitch for his mouth. Use 3 strands of black floss to make two ⅛" (3mm) single-stitch eyes. Make a brown ¼" (6mm) slanted eyebrow over each eye with 3 strands of floss. With the brown floss still attached, make a ⅜" (10mm) vertical stitch for the nose; end the nose with a ¼" (6mm) horizontal stitch (Figure 4).

4. Lay the hood back over the top of the second cotton body. Use black thread to machine-stitch along the bottom edge of the hood. Pin the front of the body to the back of the body right sides together. Machine-stitch around the outside edge, leaving a 1½" (3.8cm) opening at the base of the cotton fabric.

5. Turn the doll right-side out through the opening. Stuff him, filling the head first and then the rest of the body. Don't overstuff; he needs to fit in his castle pocket. Tuck in the cut fabric edges and hand-stitch the opening closed.

6. Pin the hat pieces right sides together and sew around 3 sides, leaving the long straight edge open. Turn right-side out and sew the feather on the front right side, leaving the top third of the feather loose (Figure 5).

Figure 4

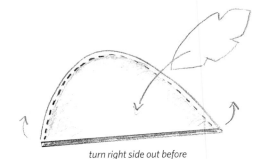

turn right side out before attaching feather

Figure 5

Aladdin's Lamp

SEWN WITH GOLD THREAD AND STUFFED WITH A GENIE SOFTIE and a lush assortment of silk scarves, this gorgeous toy is sure to spur imaginative play. A tactile toy that begs to be touched, the brocade lamp is lined with soft felt, the genie shimmers with sequins and the scarves are cool and slippery.

Note: Add ¼" (6mm) seam allowances to the indicated pattern pieces only.

Dimensions
Lamp: 12½" × 7½" × 4" (31.8cm × 19.1cm × 10.2cm)
Genie: 9½" × 5½" (24.1cm × 14cm)

MATERIALS

Lamp
Templates on page 120
1 yard (0.9cm) gold brocade
1 yard (0.9m) wool felt in gold
1 yard (0.9m) fusible interfacing
Sewing thread in coordinating
   colors

Genie
Templates on page 121
¼ yard (0.2m) wool felt in
   maroon
¼ yard (0.2m) sequined fabric
Felt scraps in skin tone, black and
   turquoise
Sewing thread in coordinating
   colors
Black embroidery floss
Fiberfill stuffing

Scarves
½ yard (0.5m) each of pink,
   turquoise and purple silk
Liquid seam sealant
Wax paper

TOOLS

Sewing machine
Iron and ironing board
Rotary cutter
Cutting mat
Ruler
Scissors
Embroidery and sewing needles
Straight pins

Lamp Instructions

1. Follow the manufacturer's instructions to iron the interfacing to the back side of the brocade. Once the interfacing is fully bonded, cut the following pattern pieces, adding a ¼" (6mm) seam allowance: 1 lid, 1 handle, 2 sides, 1 top piece, and 1 base piece.

Cut a duplicate set of lamp template pieces out of gold felt to line the lamp.

2. Pin the brocade lid to the felt lining, right sides together. Machine-stitch around the outside edge, leaving the flat end open. Clip the curves and across the point, taking care not to clip into stitching. Turn the lid right-side out, press it flat and topstitch around the rounded, stitched edge (Figure 1).

3. Pin the handle pieces right sides together. Machine-stitch around the outside edge, leaving the short flat end open. Clip curves and turn the handle right-side out. Press the handle flat and topstitch around the seamed edge (Figure 2).

4. Pair and pin the felt and brocade base pieces right sides together. Insert the lid and handle between the wide (top) ends of the base pieces, lining up all the flat ends. Check your stack: The felt side of the lid should rest against the felt base piece, the brocade side of the lid against the brocade side of the handle, and the felt side of the handle against the brocade side of the base piece. Machine-stitch the top edge of all the pieces together in a single seam (Figure 3a).

5. Working on the opposite end of the base pieces with right sides still together, line up the small ends. Make a small seam across the spout end (Figure 3b). Turn the piece right-side out and press the lid/handle connection and the spout connection flat.

6. Placing right sides together, pin a brocade side to each felt side. Make 1 seam along the top edge; that will become the lamp opening. Make a second seam across the short spout end (Figure 4). Turn the sides right-side out, and press them flat.

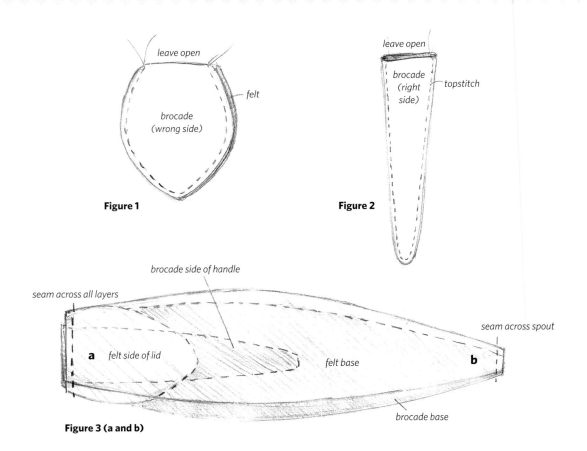

leave open

felt

brocade
(wrong side)

Figure 1

leave open

brocade
(right
side)

topstitch

Figure 2

seam across all layers

brocade side of handle

seam across spout

a felt side of lid

felt base

b

brocade base

Figure 3 (a and b)

7. Pin the brocade top piece to the felt top piece, right sides together. Make 2 separate seams to stitch the top end and spout end (Figure 5). Turn the top piece right-side out and press it flat.

8. Placing brocade sides together, pin the sides of the top piece to the top sides of the side pieces. Make 2 separate seams to join the pieces together (Figure 6).

9. Placing brocade sides together, pin the base piece to the bottom edge of the side pieces. Make a continuous seam from the top opening to the spout on either side of the lamp. Turn the lamp right-side out to make sure you've caught both the brocade and felt layers in your seam (Figure 7).

10. Use a rotary cutter, ruler and cutting mat to cut 1" (2.5cm) wide gold felt strips. Turn the lamp wrong-side out. Fold a strip over each seam and stitch it in place.

11. Turn the lamp right-side out. Hand-stitch the pointed handle end to the brocade in the center of the base piece, 4½" (11.4cm) down from the top opening.

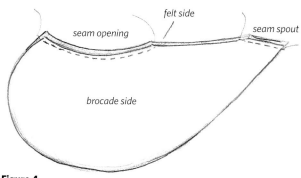

felt side

seam opening

seam spout

brocade side

Figure 4

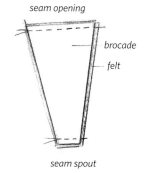

seam opening

brocade

felt

seam spout

Figure 5

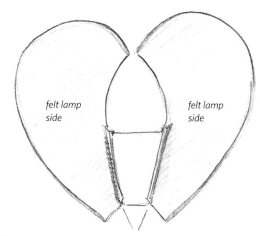

felt lamp side

felt lamp side

Figure 6

top piece, felt side

handle

lid

seam base to sides

Figure 7

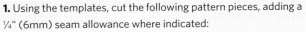

Genie

1. Using the templates, cut the following pattern pieces, adding a ¼" (6mm) seam allowance where indicated:

- From the sequined fabric, cut 1 cloud (add seam allowance).
- From the maroon felt, cut 1 cloud (add seam allowance), 1 shirt, 1 sleeve and 1 hat.
- From the skin tone felt, cut 1 body piece, 1 face piece and 1 of each forearm.
- From the turquoise felt, cut 1 feather.
- From the black felt, cut 1 mustache and 1 beard.

2. Pin the body piece to the sequined cloud and machine-stitch around the outside edge with coordinating thread.

Pin the shirt over the body and stitch it in place with coordinating thread. Pin the sleeves over the base of the shirt and sew them in place.

Pin the forearms and face piece in place and stitch them with coordinating thread.

Finally, pin the hat and feather in place and stitch them with coordinating thread.

3. Hand-stitch the genie's face. First, hand-stitch the mustache and beard in place with black sewing thread. Switch to 6 strands of black embroidery floss and an embroidery needle to make 2 French knot eyes and slanted straight-stitch eyebrows.

4. Pin the felt and sequined cloud pieces, right sides together, then machine-stitch around the outside edge, leaving a 1½" (3.8cm) opening at the base of the cloud. Turn the genie right-side out (Figure 8).

5. Push stuffing into the genie's head first, then the rest of the body, being sure to fill the narrow curved base piece. Hand-stitch the opening closed.

Scarves

1. Working over a wax-paper-covered cutting mat, use a ruler to draw a 10" (25.4cm) square on each silk color with liquid seam sealant. Wipe the ruler dry with a paper towel between each application to prevent unintentional glue transfer. Let the sealant dry completely; remove wax paper before continuing.

2. Use the rotary cutter and ruler to slice through the center of the dried sealant. Make sure all the cut edges are protected by a small line of dried sealant. Don't worry if there's not enough; you can easily reapply a thin line to the cut edge. Once dry, layer the scarves, and push them through the lamp opening.

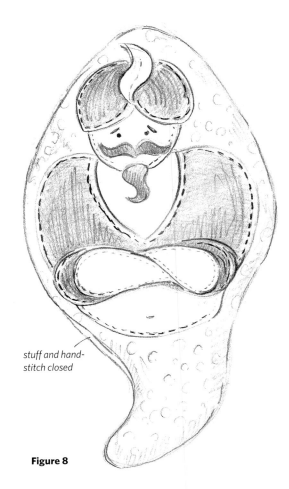

stuff and hand-stitch closed

Figure 8

Cottage Tote with Doll Sets

THE PERFECT MOBILE HOME, this little cottage is custom built for traveling adventures. The front wall easily opens and closes to create an instant play space for your favorite cast of felt characters. The fabric dictates what kind of house you build; a timber pattern for a woodland cottage fit for Snow White, or geometric squares for a classic brick home even a big bad wolf can't destroy.

 Note: Add ¼" (6mm) seam allowances to the indicated pattern pieces only.

Dimensions: 13¼" × 8" (33.7cm × 20.3cm)

MATERIALS

Templates on page 122

¼ yard (0.2m) yellow printed cotton (for roof)

¼ yard (0.2m) brown printed cotton (for exterior and interior walls)

¼ yard (0.2m) green floral printed cotton (for exterior and interior floor)

⅛ yard (0.1m) blue dot printed cotton (for the strap)

Scrap of brown cotton fabric (for the door)

Scrap of fusible web (for the door)

½ yard (0.5m) fusible fleece interfacing

18" (45.7cm) beige hook-and-loop fastener

Cardboard scrap (from a cracker or cookie box) or plastic or canvas mesh (for a washable tote)

½" (1.3cm) felt ball

Sewing thread in coordinating colors

TOOLS

Sewing machine

Iron and ironing board

Scissors (fabric and paper)

Sewing needles

Straight pins

1. Using the templates, cut the following pattern pieces, adding a ¼" (6mm) seam allowance:

- From the yellow printed cotton, cut 4 roof fronts/backs and 4 roof sides.
- From the brown printed cotton, cut 3 wall fronts/backs and 4 wall sides.
- From the green floral printed cotton, cut 1 wall front/back. Cut two 8¼" × 5½" (21cm × 14cm) rectangles for the floor.
- From the blue dot printed cotton, cut a 4½" × 10" (11.4cm × 25.4cm) strap.
- Following the manufacturer's instructions, iron the fusible web to the back side of the door scrap fabric and then cut a 3½" × 2½" (8.9cm × 6.4cm) rectangle for the door.

2. Cut the adhesive fleece lining pieces to the templates' actual size (don't add seam allowance): 2 roof fronts/backs, 2 roof sides, 2 wall fronts/backs, 2 wall sides and a 1½" × 10" (3.8cm × 25.4cm) strip for the strap.

3. Following the manufacturer's instructions, iron a fleece liner to the center back of 1 wall front and 1 wall back, 2 wall sides, 1 roof front, 1 roof back and 2 roof sides. Position the fleece strip down the length of the fabric strap, straighten it ¼" (6mm) from 1 edge, then iron it in place. These are now the exterior pieces.

4. Placing right sides together, pin the exterior roof back over the exterior wall back and the exterior roof sides over each exterior wall side. Make individual straight seams to connect the wall pieces to the roof pieces (Figure 1). Repeat with the interior pieces. Note that the front roof and front wall pieces are not sewn together.

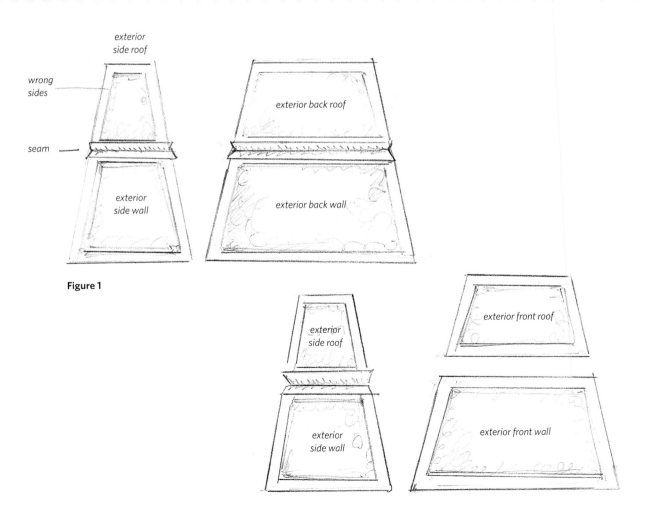

exterior side roof

wrong sides

seam

exterior side wall

exterior back roof

exterior back wall

Figure 1

exterior side roof

exterior side wall

exterior front roof

exterior front wall

5. Stitch the exterior side walls and roofs to either side of the exterior back wall and roof, connecting the 3 walls and roofs into a single piece (Figure 2). Sew the sides of the exterior front roof, right-sides together, to the exterior side roofs. Repeat the process for the interior walls/roofs.

6. Turn the interior piece right-side out. Leave the exterior piece wrong-side out. Slide the interior piece into the exterior piece, aligning the front opening. Pin the edges around the opening of the interior and exterior pieces together (up one side wall, across the bottom edge of the front roof and down the other side wall). Machine-stitch around the opening (Figure 3). Pull the connected tote sides right side out, and press the seams flat.

7. Fold and pin the length of the strap then stitch the cut edges together. Turn the strap right side out and press it flat. Topstitch either side of the strip ¼" (6mm) from the outside edge (Figure 4).

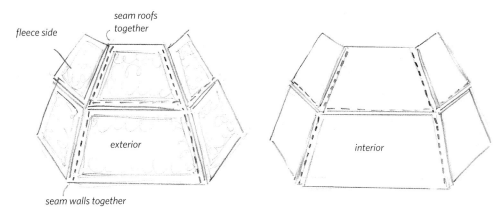

Figure 2

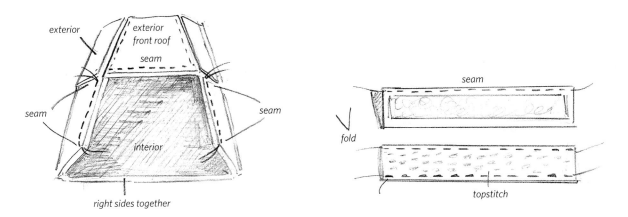

Figure 3

Figure 4

8. Insert the bottom edges of the straps into the center top front and back of the roof. Tuck in ¼" (6mm) of the roof's fabric edge and pin it in place, catching the strap ends between the layers. Topstitch around the top of the roof, trapping the strap ends in your seam (Figure 5).

9. Placing right sides together, pin the bottom edge of the interior wall (green) to 1 side of the interior floor piece. Machine-stitch them together (Figure 6).

10. Iron the door to the center bottom of the exterior front wall. Make an ⅛" (3mm) wide zigzag stitch up 1 side of the door, across the top and down the other side (Figure 7). Placing right sides together, lay the exterior front wall over the interior front

wall. Stitch around the top and sides of the front wall (Figure 8). Trim excess fabric from the corners, and turn the piece right-side out. Iron the finished front wall flat.

11. With the exterior walls facing out, line up and pin the corner seams of the exterior and interior walls together. This will ensure the tote is smooth and flat before connecting it to the floor. Pin the base of the side walls and the back wall to the base of the interior floor. Make a continuous seam around the base of all 3 walls to connect them to the floor (Figure 9).

12. Lay the exterior floor right-side down over the tote, trapping the tote walls between the layers. Line up and pin a side edge together, then stitch it. Line up and pin the back exterior floor

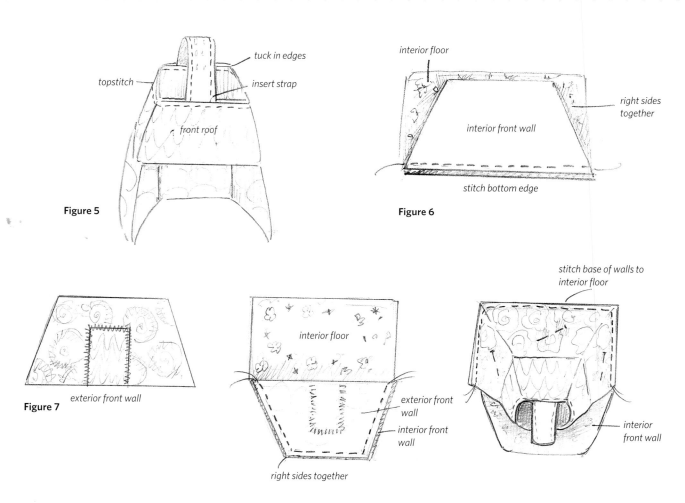

tuck in edges

topstitch

insert strap

front roof

Figure 5

interior floor

right sides together

interior front wall

stitch bottom edge

Figure 6

exterior front wall

Figure 7

interior floor

exterior front wall

interior front wall

right sides together

Figure 8

stitch base of walls to interior floor

interior front wall

Figure 9

edge with the interior floor edge, and stitch it. Repeat the process to connect the second short side edge (Figure 10). Turn the floor right-side out to check your seams, especially the corners. Make any necessary adjustments, then trim the excess fabric from the corners before turning it right-side out a final time.

13. Separate the hook-and-loop fastener. The hook portion will go around the tote opening, and the loop portion around the edge of the front wall. Position the fastener strips so they only overlap the outside edge of the tote fabric. Starting with the front wall, make a continuous seam that begins at the floor,

stop to mitre the hook fastener at each corner so it lies flat, then end your seam at the other side of the floor. Repeat the process to encircle the opening with the loop fastener (Figure 11). There's no need to fold it; just ease it around the corners.

14. Cut the cardboard or canvas into a 7¾"× 5" (19.7cm × 12.7cm) floor insert. Slide the cardboard between the fabric floor layers. Tuck ¼" (6mm) of the fabric floor edges into the opening and then hand-stitch the opening closed with small invisible stitches (Figure 12). Hand-stitch the felt ball door knob to the front door.

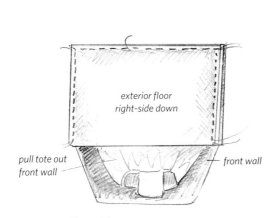

exterior floor right-side down

pull tote out front wall

front wall

Figure 10

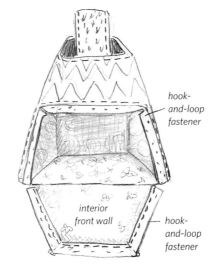

hook-and-loop fastener

interior front wall

hook-and-loop fastener

Figure 11

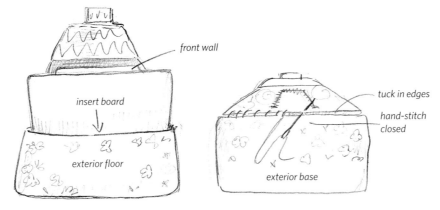

front wall

insert board

exterior floor

tuck in edges

hand-stitch closed

exterior base

Figure 12

SNOW WHITE AND
SEVEN DWARFS
MATERIALS

Templates on page 123

Wool felt in red, yellow, brown,
skin tone, white, assorted
blues, browns and greens

Sewing thread in off-white

Embroidery floss in black, white,
brown, blue, green and red

Fiberfill stuffing

TOOLS

Scissors

Sewing and embroidery needles

Dimensions
Snow White: 4½" × 3" (11.4cm × 7.6cm)
Each dwarf: 4" × 2" (10.2cm × 5.1cm)

Snow White

1. Using the templates, cut the following pattern pieces (do not add seam allowance):

- From red felt, cut 1 body and 1 cape.
- From yellow felt, cut 1 body.
- From skin tone felt, cut 1 face.
- From brown felt, cut 1 hair piece.

2. Arrange the red cape over the yellow body front, then place the face and hair over the head portion of the cape. Using sewing thread and small invisible stitches, tack the hair in place. Use 3 strands of black floss to embroider the eyes with V-stitches and French knots, and 3 strands of red floss to embroider the mouth with a V-stitch.

With 3 strands of green floss, make 7 decorative V-stitches down the front of the yellow dress. Use 3 strands of red floss to whipstitch the front body to the back (red) body, stopping to stuff Snow White before completing the seam.

Dwarf

1. Using the templates, cut the following pattern pieces (do not add seam allowance):

- From assorted felt colors, cut 14 bodies and 7 hats.
- From skin tone felt, cut 7 faces and 7 noses.
- From white felt, cut 7 beards.

2. Pin the hat, face, nose and beard to the body front. Stitch the bottom edge of the hat in place with 3 strands of a matching color of floss. Then stitch the top edge of the beard with 3 strands of white floss. Use sewing thread to tack the nose in place. Embroider the dwarf's face with 3 strands of black floss, changing the expression for each dwarf. Whipstitch the front body to the back body with a matching color of floss, stopping to stuff the dwarf before completing the seam. Repeat to make the other 6 dwarfs.

WOLF AND THREE
LITTLE PIGS
MATERIALS

Templates on pages 122, 123

Wool felt in gray, white, red,
    light-pink, dark-pink, tan, blue
    and green

Embroidery floss in black, pink,
    brown, green, blue and white

Sewing thread in white

Fiberfill stuffing

TOOLS

Scissors

Sewing and embroidery needles

Dimensions
Wolf: 4¾" × 2¼" (12.1cm × 5.7cm)
Each pig: 4¾" × 3" (12.1cm ×
7.6cm)

Wolf

1. Using the templates, cut the following pattern pieces (do not add seam allowance):

- From white felt, cut 1 body, 1 face and 1 tail.
- From gray felt, cut 1 body and 1 chest.
- From red felt, cut 1 bandana.
- From black felt, cut 1 nose.

2. Pin the chest piece over the white body and the white face over the chest piece. Tack both pieces in place using sewing thread and small invisible stitches.

Position the nose and the bandana and sew them in place. Use 3 strands of floss for all embroidery. Use black floss to embroider the mouth (with straight stitches and a *V*-stitch) and eyes (with small *V*-stitches and straight stitches). Pin the tail to the gray body piece and sew it in place with sewing thread, using small invisible stitches. Use white floss to whipstitch the white body to the gray body, stopping to stuff the wolf before you finish stitching the body shut.

Pig

1. Using the templates, cut the following pattern pieces (do not add seam allowance):

- From the light pink felt, cut 6 bodies, 6 arms and 3 tails.
- From dark pink felt, cut 3 snouts.
- From green, blue and tan felt, cut 1 each of the pants front and 1 each of the pants back.

2. Pin a pants front, 2 arms and a snout to a body front. Make a *V*-stitch at the end of each arm with 3 strands of pink floss. With 3 strands of brown floss, make a line of small straight stitches to attach the top and bottom of the pants to the front body. Make 2 small brown stitches at the bottom of the snout to hold it in place. With 3 strands of black floss and *V*-stitches, stitch the eyes and mouth.

Pin a pants back to the body back; lay the tail over the seat of the pants. With 3 strands of brown floss, make small straight stitches around the pants straps and the bottom of the pants. Sew the tail in place with sewing thread and small invisible stitches. With 3 strands of pink floss, whipstitch the front pig to the back pig, switching to a matching color of floss when you sew the pants front to the pants back. Insert stuffing before finishing sewing the pig shut. Repeat to make the other 2 pigs.

Thumbelina

TINY ENOUGH TO FIT IN A FLOWER BUD, the magical legend of Thumbelina has enchanted children for centuries. Once you've read Hans Christian Andersen's tale you may never look at a flower garden the same way, imagining fairies that flit about unseen. Sized for a child to take along on adventures, this Thumbelina doll features a removable hat and flower dress. She can hide or sleep in her leaf-pod cradle that easily bends open and closed.

 Note: Do not add seam allowances to the tempates.

Dimensions
Doll with Hat and Dress: 6¼" × 4" (15.9cm × 10.2cm)
Leaf Pod: 8" × 4½" (20.3cm × 11.4cm)

MATERIALS

Templates on page 124

Wool felt in skin tone, light-pink, cotton candy pink, white, green and yellow

Embroidery floss in white, green, yellow, pink, mustard and black

Polyester stuffing

TOOLS

Sewing machine

Scissors

Embroidery and sewing needles

Straight pins

1. Using the templates, cut out the pattern pieces (do not add seam allowances).

- From the skin tone felt, cut 2 body pieces.
- From the white felt, cut 1 hat front and 1 hat back.
- From the green felt, cut 4 leaves.
- From the yellow felt, cut 1 pod piece.
- From the light pink felt, cut 2 bunting pieces.
- From the cotton candy pink felt, cut 2 flower dresses.

2. Use 3 strands of black floss for the eyes. Each eye is made with a ¼" (6mm) horizontal stitch; don't pull the thread tight, instead bring the needle back out under the center of the stitch. Loop the floss around the first stitch and then bring the needle back down the wrong side of the work.

    Switch to 3 strands of pink thread and make two ⅛" (3.2mm) stitches to form a tiny smile. Frame her face with 3 straight stitches of hair (½" [1.3cm] to ¾" [1.9cm] long) using 3 strands of mustard floss.

3. Place a bunting piece over the bottom of the front and back body pieces. Use 3 strands of white embroidery floss and small stitches to sew the neck of the bunting to the neck of the body. Leave the floss connected to the front body piece and bring the needle back out through the front of the bunting. Make a decorative heart out of a series of small straight stitches.

4. Place and pin the front body over the back body, right-sides out. Using 3 strands of yellow floss and hiding your knot between the layers of felt at the neck, begin whipstitching the heads together.

    Continue stitching, switching to pink floss to whipstitch the bunting-covered body edges together (Figure 1). Before completely encircling the body, stop and tuck stuffing between the layers. Fill the head and body until they're full and slightly rounded, then close up the remaining opening and knot the end.

5. Using 3 strands of pink floss, make a half flower with 3 lazy daisy stitches on the hat front. Watch your tension; if you pull the last stitch too tight you'll flatten the petal. Continue using the pink floss and make a French knot flower center.

    Switch to 3 strands of green floss and make 2 connected ¼" (6mm) straight stitches on either side of the French knot. Place the finished hat front over the hat back, lining up the top of the hat and the hat sides. Using 3 strands of white floss, whipstitch the sides and top together. Leave the bottom open (Figure 2).

stuff

whipstitch

bunting

Figure 1

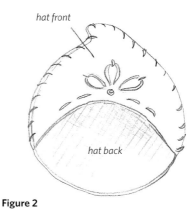

hat front

hat back

Figure 2

6. Working with 3 strands of white floss on the dress front, repeat the stitches in Step 5 to make a 3-petal lazy daisy flower with a French knot center on either side of the neckline.

Switch to 3 strands of green floss and make 4 connected ¼" (6mm) straight stitches between the flowers. Make 2 more connected straight stitches that span between the other side of the flowers and the dress shoulders. Lay the embroidered dress front over the dress back and use 3 strands of pink floss to whipstitch the dress sides together, leaving the neck opening unsewn (Figure 3).

7. Select 2 leaves to be the fronts of the leaf pod. Arrange them right-side up on your work surface, straight edges facing out and rounded sides facing in. Using 3 strands of white floss, embroider an elongated spiral that curves with the rounded edge on each leaf with ¼" (6mm) connected straight stitches beginning 2" (5.1cm) from the bottom leaf edge. Continue stitiching to form a spiral 5" (12.7cm) from the top leaf edge.

8. Stack the embroidered leaves on the plain leaves. Stretch and pin each pair of leaves along 1 side of the pod. Use 3 strands of green floss to whipstitch the straight sides of the leaves to the pod.

Working on the top side of the leaf pod, whipstitch the bottom 4" (10.2cm) of the 4 leaf tops together. Make 2 separate whip-stitch seams to connect the tops of the leaf pairs above the connection (Figure 4).

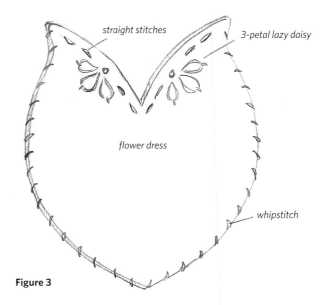

straight stitches

3-petal lazy daisy

flower dress

whipstitch

Figure 3

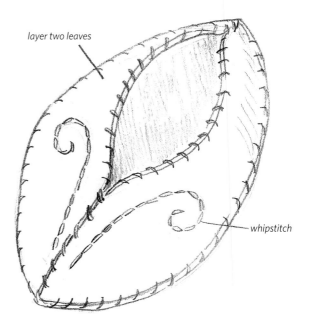

layer two leaves

whipstitch

Figure 4

Sleeping Beauty's Castle Quilt

This simple tied five-by-five block quilt requires no special piecing—the castle appears through the fabric selection. The flapping flags add dimension and fun for little fingers. The size is based on a favorite quilt from my daughters' infancy and toddler years. It fits perfectly over a car seat, makes a great travel play mat, and in a pinch works as a changing pad.

 Note: Add ¼" (6mm) seam allowances to the indicated pattern pieces.

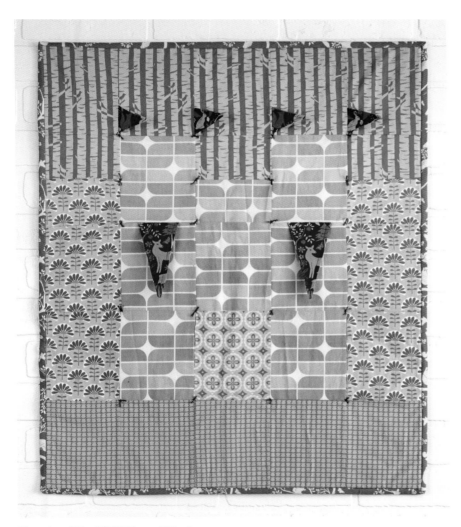

Dimensions: 28" × 23½" (71.1cm × 59.7cm)

MATERIALS

Templates on page 124

1½ yards (1.4m) natural quilt batting

1½ yards (1.4m) green flannel

½ yard (0.5m) dark-pink printed cotton (for the binding)

¼ yard (0.2m) blue printed cotton (for the background)

¼ yard (0.2m) floral printed cotton (for the sides)

¼ yard (0.2m) pink printed cotton (for the castle door)

¼ yard (0.2m) green printed cotton (for the grass)

¼ yard (0.2m) plum printed cotton (for the flags)

¼ yard (0.2m) gray printed cotton (for the castle bricks)

Embroidery floss in purple

Sewing thread in coordinating colors

TOOLS

Rotary cutter

Cutting mat

Ruler

Scissors

Sewing machine with walking foot

Straight pins

Iron and ironing board

Sewing needles

1. Cut the following pieces for the quilt top:
- Five 5" × 6" (12.7cm × 15.2cm) rectangles and three 3" × 5" (7.6cm × 12.7cm) rectangles from the blue printed background fabric.
- Seven 5" × 6" (12.7cm × 15.2cm) rectangles and one 3" × 5" (7.6cm × 12.7cm) rectangle from the gray printed fabric.
- Four 5" × 6" (12.7cm × 15.2cm) rectangles and two 3" × 5" (7.6cm × 12.7cm) rectangles from the floral printed fabric.
- One 5" × 6" (12.7cm × 15.2cm) rectangle from the pink printed fabric.
- Five 5" × 6" (12.7cm × 15.2cm) rectangles from the green printed fabric.

Use the triangle templates to cut the following, adding a ¼" (6mm) seam allowance:
- 2 large flags and 4 small flags from the plum printed fabric.
- 2 large flags and 4 small flags from the dark-pink printed fabric.

Note: Fussy cut the flag fabric to showcase a design on each flag, if desired.

2. Placing right sides together, pair a plum flag piece to each dark-pink flag piece. Machine-stitch the diagonal sides, leaving the small straight side open. Clip the extra fabric off the pointed ends, and turn the flags right-side out. If necessary, use a knitting needle to push out the pointed ends. Iron the flags flat and topstitch the seamed edges.

3. Placing right sides together, pin and stitch 1 long side of a small blue background rectangle to 1 long side of each small floral rectangle. Then pin and stitch a small gray castle rectangle to the remaining small background rectangle. Three full-size rectangles have been made (see Quilt Diagram on page 95). Press the rectangles flat.

4. Placing right sides together, pin together the 6" (15.2cm) side of 2 large blue background rectangles. Trap a small flag between the layers ⅜" (10mm) from the bottom edge, and line up the unsewn flat edge of the flag with the outside edge of the background pieces. Make a straight seam, catching the flag in your seam (Figure 1). Repeat the process to add the 3 remaining small flags and large background rectangles to finish the row.

5. Placing right sides together, stitch the second row, which includes the 3 joined half rectangles. Working left to right, pin the 6" (15.2cm) side of a joined background/floral rectangle to the 6" (15.2cm) side of a gray castle rectangle and stitch

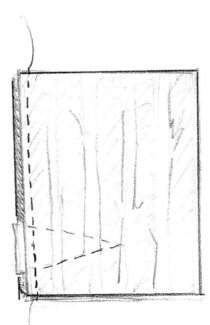

trap flag between layers

Figure 1

them together. Stitch the joined background/castle rectangle to the open side of the castle piece. Add another full castle piece and end the row with the second joined background/floral rectangle (see Quilt Diagram).

6. Lay out the third row: a floral rectangle on each side and 3 castle rectangles in the middle. Working left to right and pinning right sides together, stitch the 6" (15.2cm) sides of all 5 rectangles together to form the strip (see Quilt Diagram).

7. Lay out the fourth row: a floral rectangle on each end and 2 castle rectangles on either side with the castle door in the center. Working left to right and pinning right sides together, seam the 6" (15.2cm) sides together to form the strip (see Quilt Diagram).

8. Lay out the fifth and final row: 5 grass rectangles. Working left to right and pinning right sides together, seam the 6" (15.2cm) sides together to form the strip (see Quilt Diagram).

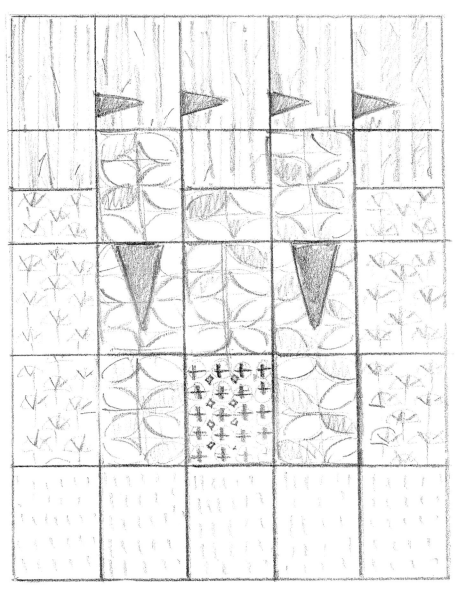

Quilt Diagram

9. Press open the seams of all 5 rows so they are smooth and flat. Connect the base of the first row to the top of the second row: Placing right sides together, line up the seams from both rows, then pin them together. Stitch a continuous seam to connect the blocks.

10. Join the base of the second row to the top of the third row, catching the long flags in your seam: Placing right sides together, insert the flags pointed ends down. Center each flag in the middle of the outer castle rectangles. Line up the unsewn flat edge of the flags with the outside edges of the castle fabric. Stitch a continuous seam to connect the blocks and trap the flags.

11. Connect the fourth and fifth rows as you did in Step 9, and press all the seams flat. Check the back side of quilt top. Trim away any excess fabric from the flags or selvedge bulk from the corners. Press all the seams open and flat.

12. Working over your cutting mat, first lay the green flannel right-side down and smooth it flat. Stack the batting over the flannel, and then top the stack with your finished quilt top. Use the rotary cutter and ruler to trim the batting and backing ½" (1.3cm) from the edge of the quilt top. Pin through all 3 layers on each rectangle to hold all of the sandwiched quilt layers together.

13. Using the rotary cutter, ruler and cutting mat, cut 2½" (6.4cm) strips of binding fabric. Overlap the strip ends perpendicular to each other (45° angle) and then machine-stitch them together. Trim away the excess and press the seam flat (Figure 2). The resulting diagonal connection will help reduce bulk. You'll need a continuous 108" (2.7m) long binding strip for your quilt. Press and fold the entire length of the strip to reduce the width to 1¼" (3.2cm).

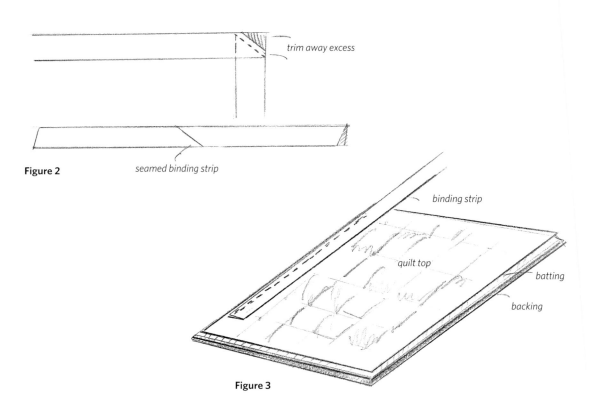

trim away excess

Figure 2   *seamed binding strip*

binding strip

quilt top

batting

backing

Figure 3

14. Install your sewing machine's walking foot (it does a great job feeding multiple layers through the machine). Begin your seam 8" (20.3cm) from a corner, leaving a 4" (10.2cm) binding tail, and stitch the open-edges side of the binding strip to the quilt edge (Figure 3). The folded width of the strip should extend over the quilt top. Stitch to within a ¼" (6mm) of the next corner. Stop the seam and fold the binding up perpendicular to the seam you just stitched (Figure 4). Fold the binding back down, aligning the edges with the seam you just sewed (Figure 5).

Start a new seam through the open end of the binding on the other side of the corner. Continue working in this fashion until you're 4" (10.2cm) from the beginning of your seam. Bring binding ends together and mark where they should be joined to cover the gap. Unfold the ends, seam them on the diagonal, and trim away the excess fabric (Figure 6). Lay the connected ends back over the quilt top and complete your binding seam.

15. Wrap the folded edge of the binding around to the back side of the quilt and hand-stitch it in place. Use small invisible stitches to join the folded edge of the binding to the quilt back. When you reach the corners, fold the additional fabric binding so one side lies flat over the other, creating a mitred corner.

16. Secure the layers by tying the quilt. Using 6 strands of floss, bring the needle through the front of the quilt where 4 corners meet. Leave a tail on the front of the quilt, then make a cross-stitch, bringing your needle through each of the corners. Tie the ends of the floss on the front side of the quilt in a double knot. Repeat the process to tie all 16 interior block connections. In the second row of the quilt, tie the 4 connections where the half rectangles join the side of a full rectangle. Trim the ends of the floss 1" (2.5cm) from the knot.

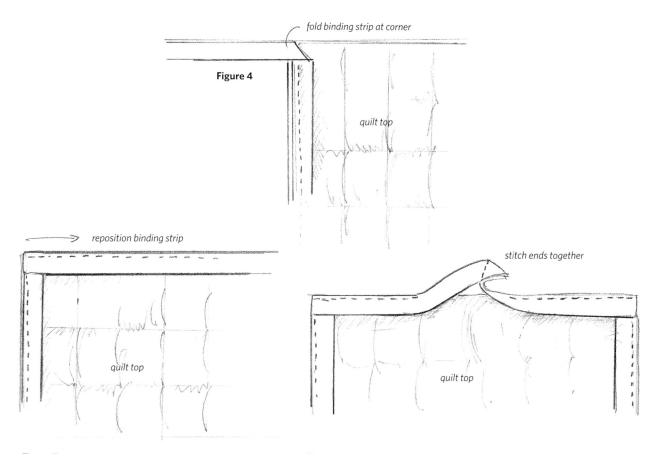

fold binding strip at corner

Figure 4

quilt top

reposition binding strip

stitch ends together

quilt top

quilt top

Figure 5

Figure 6

The Princess and the Pea Playset

PLAYING PRINCESS AND PUTTING DOLLS TO BED are favorite games for many children. This charming playset combines both. All the props for reenacting this classic story are contained in the carrying bag for easy storage.

Note: Add a ¼" (6mm) seam allowance to the indicated pattern pieces only.

MATERIALS

Princess

Templates on page 125

¼ yard (0.2m) each of 2 printed cottons (for 2 nightgowns)

¼ yard (0.2m) beige linen

⅓ yard (0.3m) fusible fleece interfacing

Pink bias tape

Pink and blue rickrack

White mini-rickrack

Embroidered trim

Orange cotton yarn

Fiberfill stuffing

Embroidery floss in black, beige, light-blue and red

Scrap of gold wool felt

Sewing thread in coordinating colors

Bedding

¼ yard (0.2m) each of 7 printed cottons (for the mattresses, blanket and pillow)

¼ yard (0.2m) white plush polyester fabric (for blanket lining)

Rolled polyester batting

Green felt ball

Short length of silk cording

Fiberfill stuffing

Sewing thread in coordinating colors

Carrying Tote

⅓ yard (0.3m) each of 2 printed cottons (for the bag and bag lining)

Two 24" (61cm) lengths of green 1" (2.5cm) grosgrain ribbon

Sewing thread in coordinating colors

Liquid seam sealant

Dimensions: 28" × 23½" (71.1cm × 59.7cm)

TOOLS

Rotary cutter

Ruler

Cutting mat

Scissors

Sewing machine

Straight pins and safety pins

Iron and ironing board

Embroidery and sewing needles

Stuffing stick

Princess Doll

1. Using the templates, cut out the following pattern pieces:

- From the linen, cut 2 body pieces, 4 arms and 4 legs adding a ¼" (6mm) seam allowance to each piece.
- From the fusible fleece interfacing, cut 2 bodies, 4 arms (flip the template and cut 2 in reverse) and 4 legs (cut 2 in reverse) (no seam allowance).
- From the felt scrap, cut the crown (no seam allowance).

2. Center a fleece lining on the back of each body, arm and leg piece. Follow the manufacturer's instructions to iron the fleece linings in place.

3. Embroider the face on the head of the front body piece using 3 strands of embroidery floss. With black floss, make an inverted, elongated ⅜" (10mm) V-stitch for the top of each eye. Make an ⅛" (3mm) vertical straight stitch down from the center of each eye for the pupils. Frame the outside edge of each eye with two ⅛" (3mm) eyelashes. Switch to light-blue floss and make a stitch on either side of each pupil.

With beige floss, make two ⅜" (10mm) connected eyebrow stitches over each eye and a single ⅛" (3mm) horizontal stitch for the nose. Make the mouth with red floss. The upper lip is formed by 2 connected triangles: The 4 slanted triangle topstitches are ⅛" (3mm) and the bases of the triangles are ¼" (6mm). Stack 2 straight stitches for the lower lip: The topstitch is ⅜" (10mm) and the lower stitch is ⅛" (3mm) (Figure 1).

4. Pair the arms and legs right sides together. Machine-stitch around the outside edge of each pair, leaving the top edge unsewn. Use a stuffing stick to turn each limb right-side out. Push stuffing into the hands and feet first, then fill the rest of the arms and legs (Figure 2).

5. Placing right sides together, stack a single body piece over the other. Insert the open arm ends between the shoulders. Pin the body pieces together, pinning the arm pieces in place, making sure only the shoulder ends will be caught in the seam. Machine-stitch up 1 side of the body, around the head, and down the other side of the body, catching the arms in your seam. Leave the bottom edge of the body open and unsewn (Figure 3). Turn the body right-side out and fill the chest and belly with stuffing.

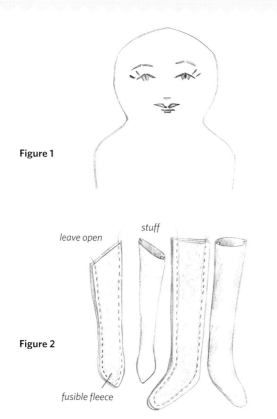

Figure 1

leave open

stuff

Figure 2

fusible fleece

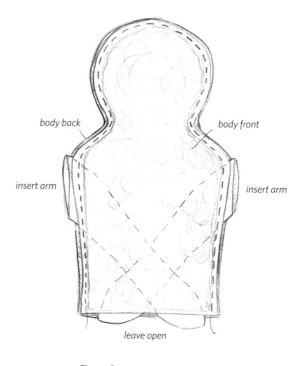

body back

body front

insert arm

insert arm

leave open

Figure 3

6. Fold up the bottom raw edge of the body, then insert the legs side by side, seam sides forward, into the opening. Securely join the the legs and body together as you hand-stitch the opening closed (Figure 4).

7. Wind the cotton yarn around a thin 10" (25.4cm) book until you're pleased with the thickness. Slide the yarn off and tie a yarn scrap around the center to form the hair part. Cut through the yarn at the untied end.

Hand-stitch the center part to the top of the head. Separate the yarn into 3 sections on both sides of the part. Start braiding each grouping, loosening the beginning of the section that is closest to the back of the head. Once you've finished braiding, wrap and tie each end with a yarn scrap. Evenly trim the yarn ends 1" (2.5cm) from the wrap ties. Hand-stitch some of the yarn strands from the loosened braid portion to the back of the head (Figure 5).

8. Fold the crown in half, lining up the crown points. Whipstitch around the 4 crown points with matching floss to join the felt layers together. Sew the flat bottom sides of the crown together to form the circle (Figure 6). While the thread is still attached, sew the base of the crown to the center top of the princess's head.

9. Using the templates, cut the following nightgown pieces, adding ¼" (6mm) seam allowances:
- From printed cotton of your choice, cut 1 sleeveless nightgown front and 2 sleeveless nightgown backs.
- From a coordinating printed cotton, cut 1 long-sleeved nightgown front and 2 long-sleeved nightgown backs.

10. Pin the sleeveless nightgown backs right sides together. Start your seam 1½" (3.8cm) from the top. This neck opening will make dressing and undressing easy. Stitch the 2 backs together. Working on the wrong side, fold over and press ¼" (6mm) of the fabric along the neck opening. Fold and press the armpit openings on both the front and back pieces. Stitch the folds in place. Repeat this step with the long-sleeved nightgown backs, folding and stitching the hems of the sleeves instead of the armpit openings.

11. Placing right sides together, pin the sleeveless nightgown back to the sleeveless nightgown front. Make a short seam at the shoulder and a second seam from the armpit down the length of the skirt. Repeat the seams on the other side of the dress.

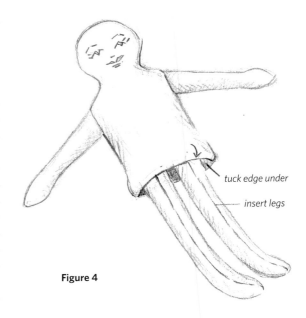

tuck edge under

insert legs

Figure 4

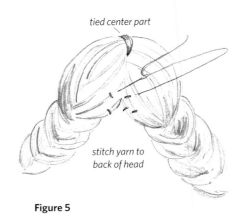

tied center part

stitch yarn to back of head

Figure 5

whipstitch

sew ends together

Figure 6

12. Placing right sides together, pin the long-sleeved nightgown front to the long-sleeved nightgown back. Make a seam starting at the shoulder and sewing down the top of the sleeve. Make a second seam starting at the underside of the sleeve and sewing up around the armpit and down the length of the skirt. Repeat the seams on the other side of the dress.

13. Stitch the bias tape to the necks of the dresses. Leaving a 5" (12.7cm) tail on either end, trap the neck of long-sleeve nightgown between the layers of the tape. The additional length on either side becomes the dress ties. Stitch through the bottom edge of the bias tape catching the fabric in your stitches. Repeat with the remaining nightgown.

14. Fold and press a ¼" (6mm) hem along the bottom edge of each nightgown. Pin the blue rickrack and trim over the folded edge on the sleeveless nightgown and the pink rickrack with the mini-rickrack on the long-sleeved nightgown. Topstitch the trim, rickrack and hemmed fabric in a single seam, overlapping and turning back the top layers of trim as they meet (Figure 7).

Bedding

1. Cut the following pieces for the box mattress:
- From printed cotton, cut two 11½" × 6½" (29.2cm × 16.5cm) rectangles for the top and bottom, two 1¾" × 11½" (4.4cm × 29.2cm) rectangles for the long sides and two 1¾" × 6½" (4.4cm × 16.5cm) rectangles for the short sides.

- From the fleece interfacing, cut two 11" × 6" (27.9cm × 15.2cm) rectangles, two 1¼" × 11" (3.2cm × 27.9cm) rectangles and two 1¼" × 6" (3.2cm × 15.2cm) rectangles.

2. Follow the manufacturer's instructions to fuse an interfacing piece to the center of each of the cotton pieces.

3. Seam the side pieces together into a single long strip: Placing right sides together, seam a short end of a short side piece to a short end of a long side piece. Seam the short end of the second short side piece to other end of the long side piece. Finish the strip by adding the second long side piece to the end of the second short side piece. Seam the the open short end and open long end together to join the strip into a rectangle.

4. Placing right sides together, line up the edges of the connected side piece with the edges of the mattress bottom. Make 4 separate seams to connect the sides to the mattress bottom 1 side at a time.

5. Repeat the process to connect the mattress top to the other edge of the side piece: Placing right sides together, make 4 more seams around the top of the box mattress. Leave a 2" (5.1cm) opening at the end of the last long seam (Figure 8). Turn the mattress right-side out through the opening.

press and stitch neck edge
seam shoulder
turn under and stitch
turn under and stitch
seam
long sleeve
sleeveless
trim

Figure 7

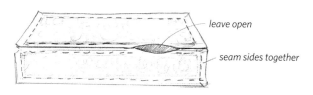

leave open
seam sides together

Figure 8

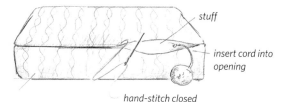

stuff
insert cord into opening
hand-stitch closed

Figure 9

6. Feed stuffing through the opening to fill the mattress. Tie a knot in 1 end of the silk cording and thread your embroidery needle. Pierce the felt ball with the needle, and pull the cording all the way through until the knot is flush with the felt. Bring the needle back through the felt ball. Then bring the needle through the inner fabric edge in the mattress opening. Leave a 2" (5.1cm) piece of cording between the bead and the mattress; knot and trim away the remaining cording (Figure 9). Tuck in the fabric edges around the opening, and switch to a sewing needle and thread to hand-stitch the opening closed.

7. Using assorted printed cottons, make at least 4 of these flat mattresses: For each mattress, cut two 11½" × 6½" (29.2cm × 16.5cm) rectangles from printed cotton and one 11" × 6" (27.9cm × 15.2cm) rectangle of rolled polyester batting.

8. Placing right sides together, pin the mattress pieces together. Stitch around the outside edge of the pieces, leaving a 3" (7.6cm) opening between the beginning and end of your seam (Figure 10). Turn the mattress right-side out through the opening. Feed the batting into the opening, adjusting so that it lies flat inside the mattress (Figure 11). Tuck in the fabric edges, and hand-stitch the opening closed.

9. To make the blanket, cut a 9¼" × 8¾" (23.5cm × 22.2cm) rectangle from printed cotton and white plush polyester fabric. Pair and pin the pieces right sides together. Make a continuous seam around the outside edge leaving a 2" (5.1cm) opening between the beginning and end of the seam. Trim the corners, then pull the blanket right-side out through the opening. While you press the blanket flat, tuck in the edges at the opening. Topstitch around the outside edge ¼" (6mm) from the seamed edge.

10. To make the pillow, cut two 3¾" × 5¾" (9.5cm × 14.6cm) rectangles from printed cotton. Pair and pin the pieces right sides together. Machine-stitch around the outside edge, leaving a 1½" (3.8cm) opening. Trim the corners and turn the pillow right-side out. Push stuffing into the opening, tuck in the open edges and hand-stitch the opening closed.

wrong side   *leave open*

Figure 10

stretch stuffing into corners   *insert batting*

Figure 11

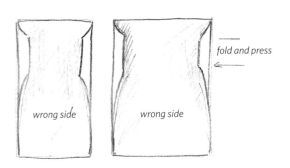

fold and press

wrong side   *wrong side*

Figure 12

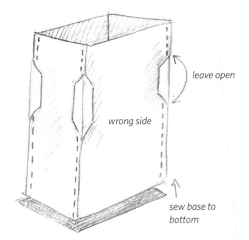

leave open

wrong side

sew base to bottom

Figure 13

Carrying Tote

1. Cut the following pieces for the tote:

From each of the 2 printed cottons, cut two 14½" × 7½" (36.8cm × 19.1cm) rectangles for the front and back, two 14½" × 5" (36.8cm × 12.7cm) rectangles for the sides and one 7½" × 5" (19.1cm × 12.7cm) rectangle for the base.

2. Working with the exterior fabric, fold under and press ¼" (6mm) of the fabric edge for a 2" (5.1cm) section, and 1¾" (4.4cm) from the top on the front, back and side pieces to make a drawstring opening (Figure 12). Placing right sides together, pin the side pieces between the front and back pieces. Stitch the edges together in 4 separate seams, interrupting each seam at the 2" (5.1cm) drawstring openings.

3. Insert the exterior base piece right-side down over the bottom opening, pin and then stitch it in place with a continuous seam (Figure 13). Turn the tote right-side out.

4. To make the lining, seam the front, back and side lining pieces right sides together, then stitch the lining base to the bottom.

5. Placing right sides together, insert the lining into the exterior of the tote (Figure 14). Line up and pin the top edges together. Machine-stitch all the way around the top of the tote. Leave a 2" (5.1cm) opening between the beginning and end of the seam (Figure 15). Turn the bag right-side out through the opening and settle the lining into the tote. Tuck in and press the fabric edges at the opening. Topstitch ¼" (6mm) from the seamed edge all the way around the top of the tote.

6. Topstitch around both layers at the top and bottom of the drawstring opening to create a casing for the drawstring.

7. Hook a safety pin to the ribbon end and feed it through left to right across the front of the tote. Bring it across the outside of the side panel, then feed it right to left across the back panel. Remove the pin and tie the ends together in an overhand knot. Repeat the process in the opposite direction with the second ribbon length (Figure 16). To help prevent the ribbon from fraying, apply a bead of liquid seam sealant to the cut ends.

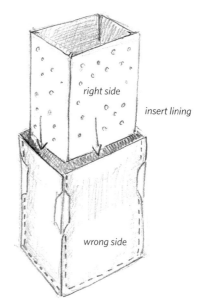

right side

insert lining

wrong side

Figure 14

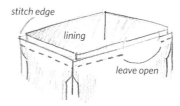

stitch edge

lining

leave open

Figure 15

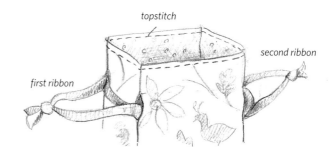

topstitch

second ribbon

first ribbon

Figure 16

Templates

Troll Templates: Enlarge all pieces at 400%

Base
Cut 1 from cotton
Add ¼" (6mm) seam allowance

Body Front
Cut 1 from beige fleece
Add ¼" (6mm) seam allowance

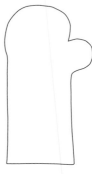

Arm
Cut 4 from beige fleece
Add ¼" (6mm) seam allowance

Attach to other body back piece

Attach to front piece

Nose
Cut 2 from beige fleece
Add ¼" (6mm) seam
allowance

Tooth
Cut 2 from white felt
Add ¼" (6mm) seam
allowance

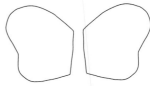

Ears
Cut 1 set each from beige and
brown fleece
Add ¼" (6mm) seam allowance

Body Back
Cut 2 from beige fleece
Add ¼" seam allowance

Pant Back
Cut 2 from cotton
Add ¼" (6mm) seam allowance

Inside edge

Outside edge

Pant Front
Cut 2 from cotton
Add ¼" (6mm) seam allowance

Feet
Cut 1 set each from beige and brown fleece
Add ¼" (6mm) seam allowance

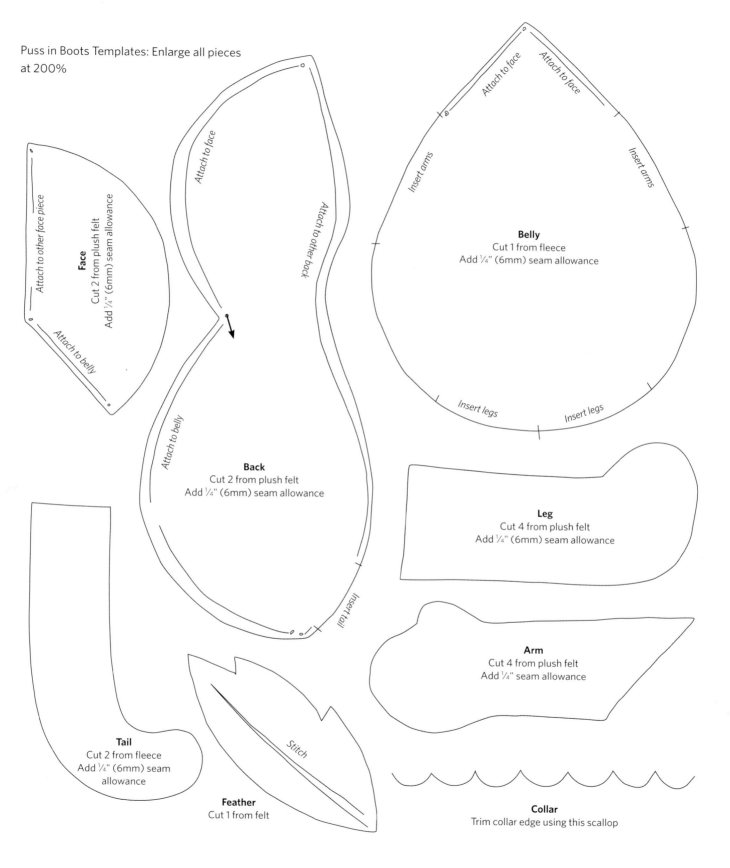

Puss in Boots Templates: Enlarge all pieces at 200%

Face
Cut 2 from plush felt
Add ¼" (6mm) seam allowance

Attach to face

Attach to other face piece

Attach to belly

Attach to face

Attach to other back

Attach to belly

Back
Cut 2 from plush felt
Add ¼" (6mm) seam allowance

Insert tail

Belly
Cut 1 from fleece
Add ¼" (6mm) seam allowance

Attach to face

Attach to face

Insert arms

Insert arms

Insert legs

Insert legs

Leg
Cut 4 from plush felt
Add ¼" (6mm) seam allowance

Arm
Cut 4 from plush felt
Add ¼" seam allowance

Tail
Cut 2 from fleece
Add ¼" (6mm) seam allowance

Feather
Cut 1 from felt

Stitch

Collar
Trim collar edge using this scallop

Puss in Boots Templates, continued: Enlarge all pieces at 200%

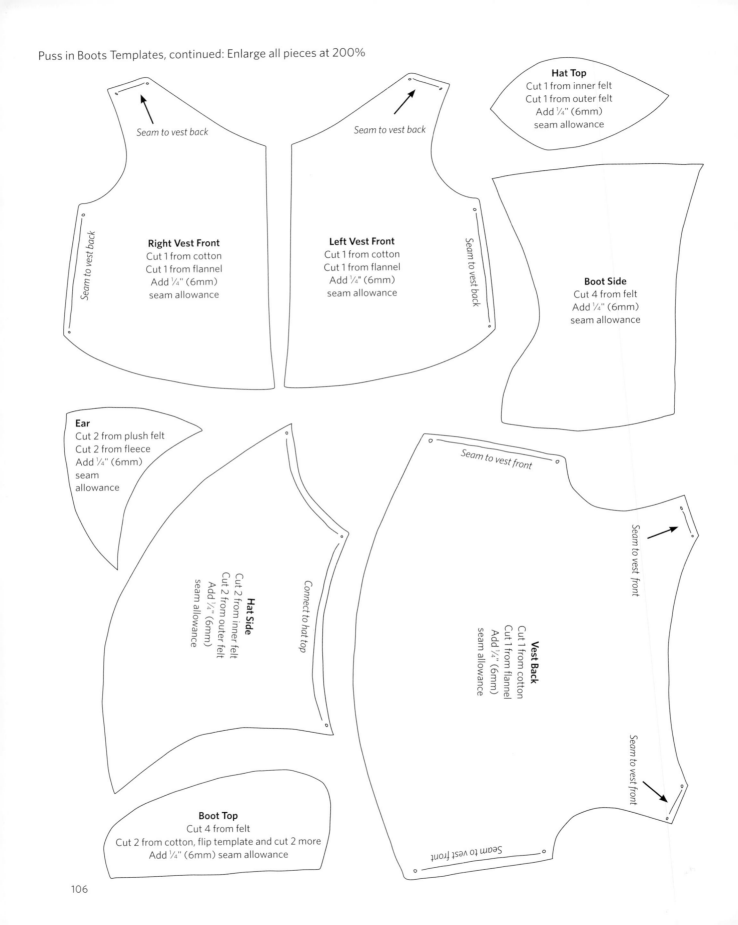

Seam to vest back

Seam to vest back

Seam to vest back

Seam to vest back

Right Vest Front
Cut 1 from cotton
Cut 1 from flannel
Add ¼" (6mm)
seam allowance

Left Vest Front
Cut 1 from cotton
Cut 1 from flannel
Add ¼" (6mm)
seam allowance

Hat Top
Cut 1 from inner felt
Cut 1 from outer felt
Add ¼" (6mm)
seam allowance

Boot Side
Cut 4 from felt
Add ¼" (6mm)
seam allowance

Ear
Cut 2 from plush felt
Cut 2 from fleece
Add ¼" (6mm)
seam
allowance

Hat Side
Cut 2 from inner felt
Cut 2 from outer felt
Add ¼" (6mm)
seam allowance

Connect to hat top

Seam to vest front

Seam to vest front

Seam to vest front

Vest Back
Cut 1 from cotton
Cut 1 from flannel
Add ¼" (6mm)
seam allowance

Boot Top
Cut 4 from felt
Cut 2 from cotton, flip template and cut 2 more
Add ¼" (6mm) seam allowance

Seam to vest front

Little Mermaid Templates: Enlarge all pieces at 200%

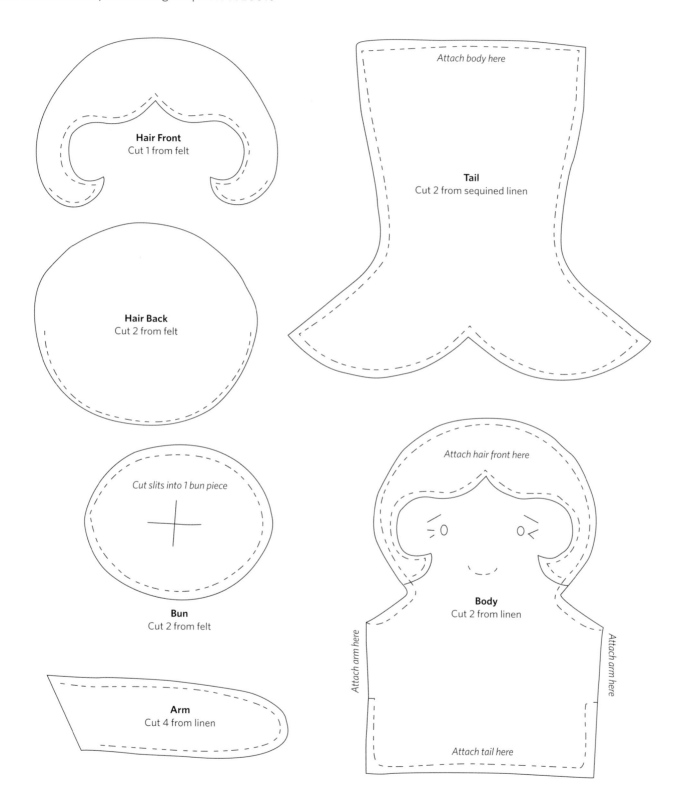

Hair Front
Cut 1 from felt

Hair Back
Cut 2 from felt

Cut slits into 1 bun piece

Bun
Cut 2 from felt

Arm
Cut 4 from linen

Attach body here

Tail
Cut 2 from sequined linen

Attach hair front here

Body
Cut 2 from linen

Attach arm here

Attach arm here

Attach tail here

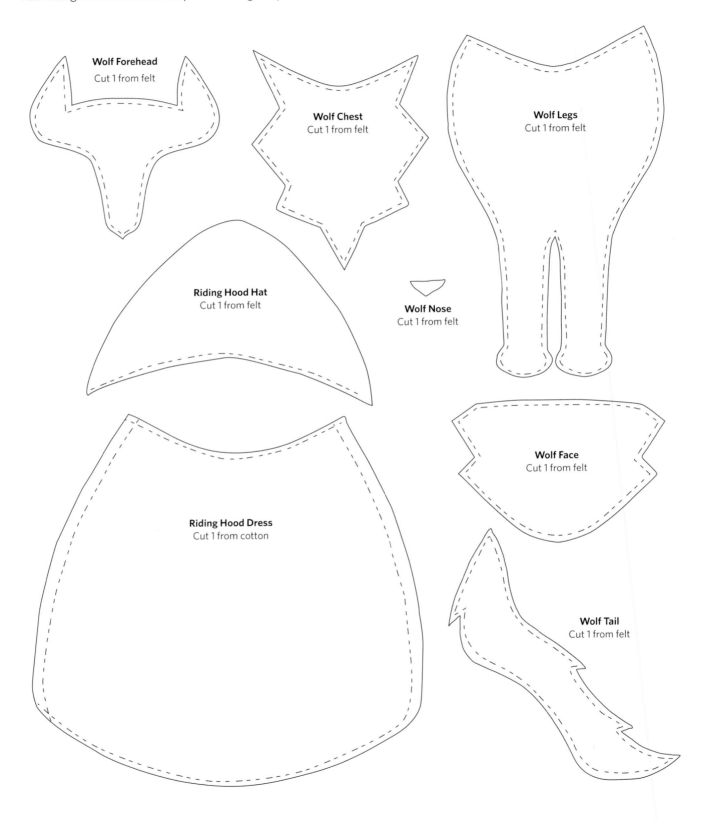

Wolf Forehead
Cut 1 from felt

Wolf Chest
Cut 1 from felt

Wolf Legs
Cut 1 from felt

Riding Hood Hat
Cut 1 from felt

Wolf Nose
Cut 1 from felt

Riding Hood Dress
Cut 1 from cotton

Wolf Face
Cut 1 from felt

Wolf Tail
Cut 1 from felt

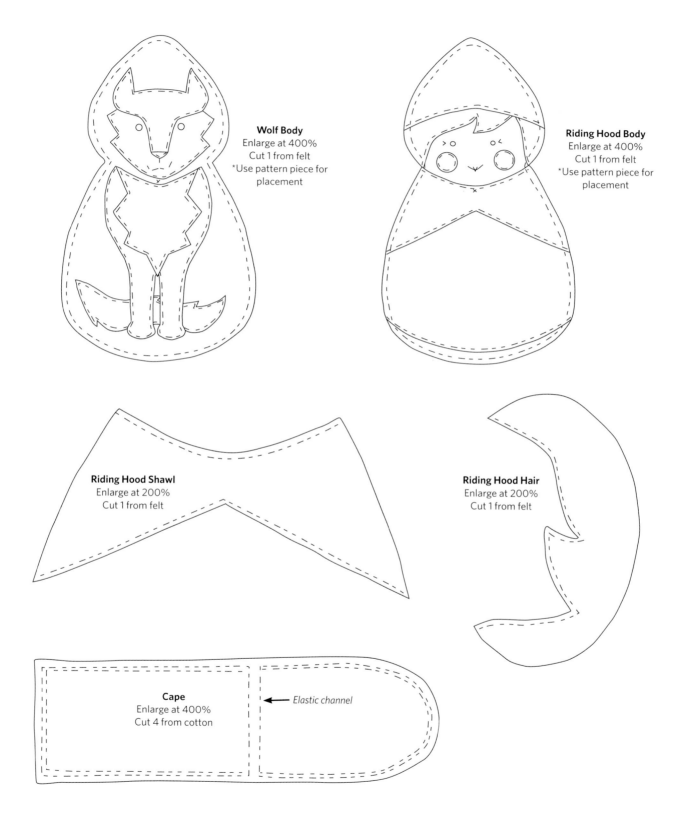

Wolf Body
Enlarge at 400%
Cut 1 from felt
*Use pattern piece for placement

Riding Hood Body
Enlarge at 400%
Cut 1 from felt
*Use pattern piece for placement

Riding Hood Shawl
Enlarge at 200%
Cut 1 from felt

Riding Hood Hair
Enlarge at 200%
Cut 1 from felt

Cape
Enlarge at 400%
Cut 4 from cotton

← *Elastic channel*

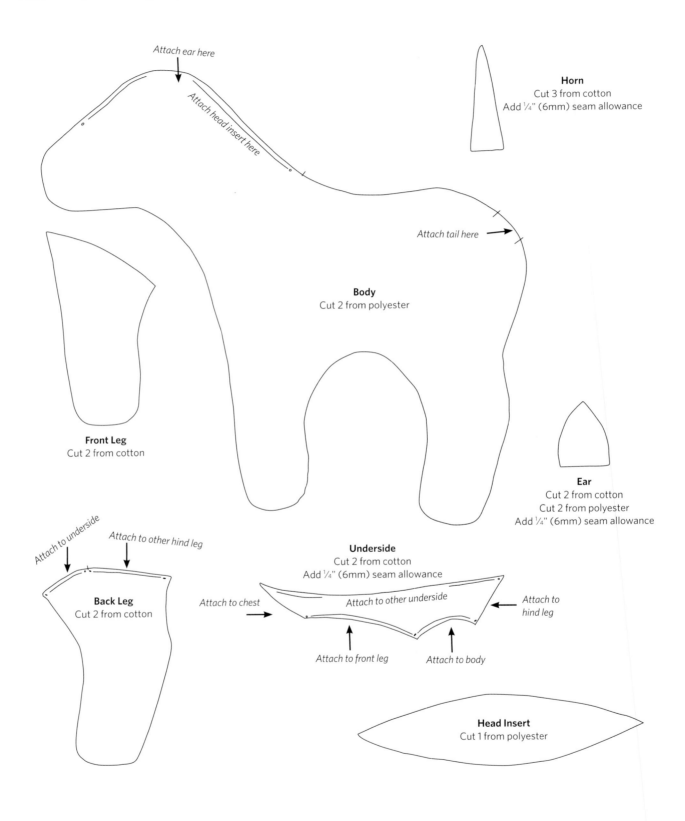

Attach ear here

Attach head insert here

Attach tail here

Body
Cut 2 from polyester

Front Leg
Cut 2 from cotton

Horn
Cut 3 from cotton
Add ¼" (6mm) seam allowance

Ear
Cut 2 from cotton
Cut 2 from polyester
Add ¼" (6mm) seam allowance

Attach to underside

Attach to other hind leg

Back Leg
Cut 2 from cotton

Underside
Cut 2 from cotton
Add ¼" (6mm) seam allowance

Attach to chest

Attach to other underside

Attach to hind leg

Attach to front leg

Attach to body

Head Insert
Cut 1 from polyester

Shoemaker's Elves Templates: Enlarge all pieces at 200%

Body
Cut 2 per elf from felt

Dress/Shirt
Cut 2 per elf from felt

Arm
Cut 4 per elf from felt

Leg
Cut 4 per elf from felt

Vest Back
Cut 1 from felt

Boy Hair Front
Cut 1 from felt

Boy Hair Back
Cut 1 from felt

Boy Hat
Cut 2 from felt

Vest Front
Cut 2 from felt

Girl Hair Front
Cut 1 from felt

Girl Hat Front
Cut 1 from felt

Feather
Cut 1 from felt

Girl Hair Back
Cut 2 from felt

Dress Trim
Cut 2 from felt

Girl Hat Back
Cut 1 from felt

Bow
Cut 1 from felt

Apron
Cut 1 from felt

Heart
Cut 1 from felt

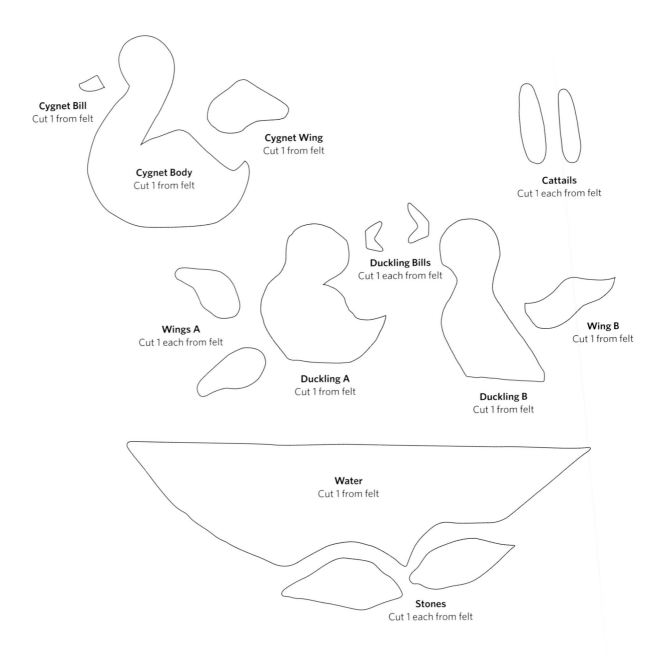

Cygnet Bill
Cut 1 from felt

Cygnet Wing
Cut 1 from felt

Cygnet Body
Cut 1 from felt

Cattails
Cut 1 each from felt

Duckling Bills
Cut 1 each from felt

Wings A
Cut 1 each from felt

Wing B
Cut 1 from felt

Duckling A
Cut 1 from felt

Duckling B
Cut 1 from felt

Water
Cut 1 from felt

Stones
Cut 1 each from felt

Frog Prince Templates: All pieces shown at 100%

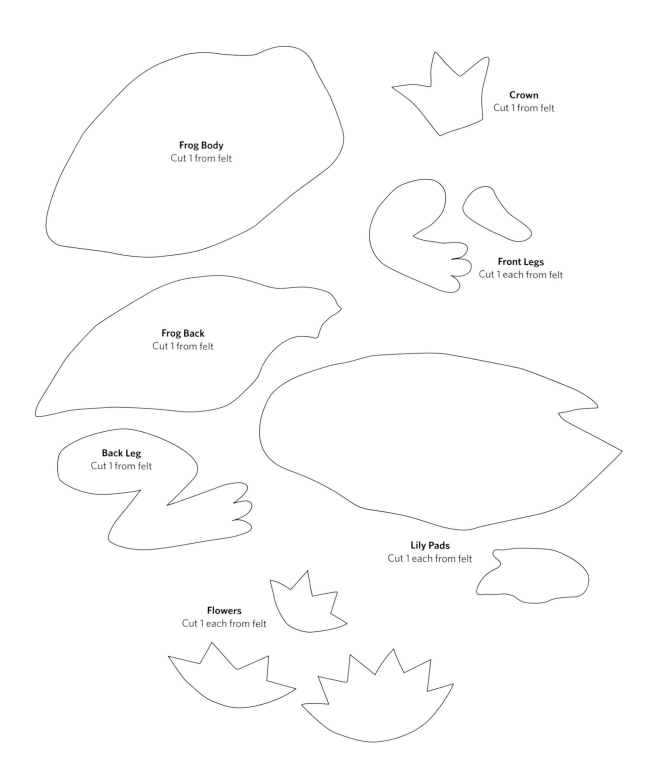

Frog Body
Cut 1 from felt

Crown
Cut 1 from felt

Front Legs
Cut 1 each from felt

Frog Back
Cut 1 from felt

Back Leg
Cut 1 from felt

Lily Pads
Cut 1 each from felt

Flowers
Cut 1 each from felt

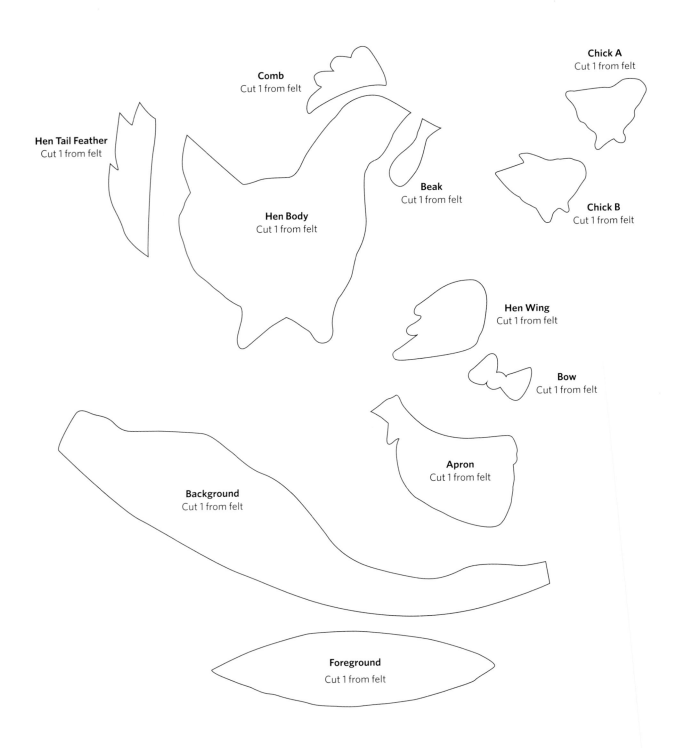

Comb
Cut 1 from felt

Chick A
Cut 1 from felt

Hen Tail Feather
Cut 1 from felt

Beak
Cut 1 from felt

Chick B
Cut 1 from felt

Hen Body
Cut 1 from felt

Hen Wing
Cut 1 from felt

Bow
Cut 1 from felt

Apron
Cut 1 from felt

Background
Cut 1 from felt

Foreground
Cut 1 from felt

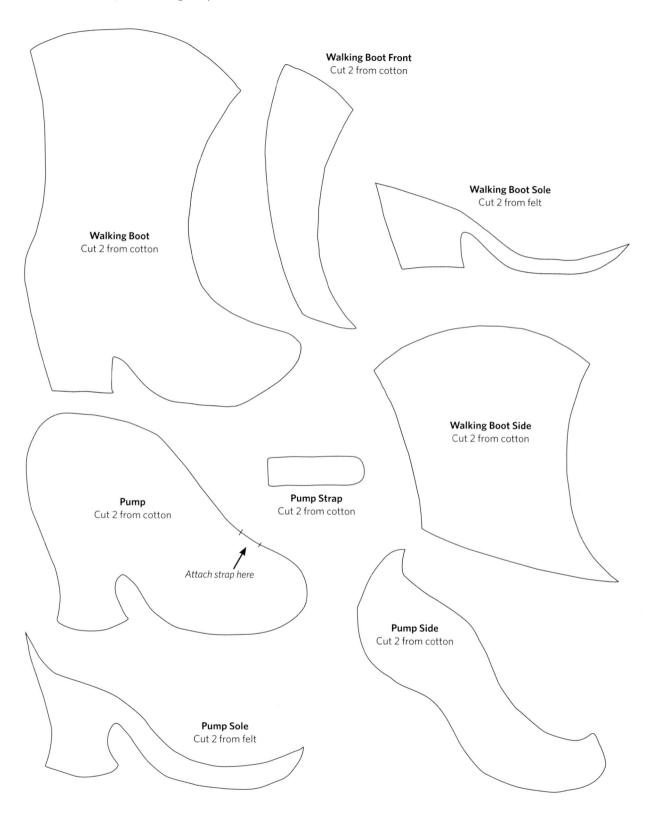

Walking Boot Front
Cut 2 from cotton

Walking Boot Sole
Cut 2 from felt

Walking Boot
Cut 2 from cotton

Walking Boot Side
Cut 2 from cotton

Pump
Cut 2 from cotton

Pump Strap
Cut 2 from cotton

Attach strap here

Pump Side
Cut 2 from cotton

Pump Sole
Cut 2 from felt

Cinderella's Shoes Templates: Enlarge all pieces at 400%

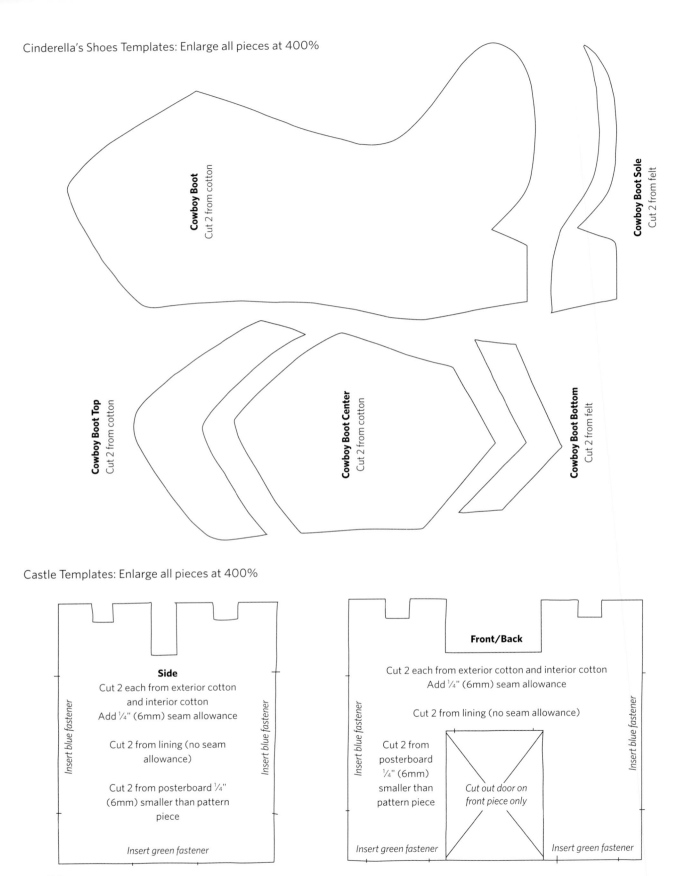

Cowboy Boot
Cut 2 from cotton

Cowboy Boot Sole
Cut 2 from felt

Cowboy Boot Top
Cut 2 from cotton

Cowboy Boot Center
Cut 2 from cotton

Cowboy Boot Bottom
Cut 2 from felt

Castle Templates: Enlarge all pieces at 400%

Side
Cut 2 each from exterior cotton
and interior cotton
Add ¼" (6mm) seam allowance

Cut 2 from lining (no seam
allowance)

Cut 2 from posterboard ¼"
(6mm) smaller than pattern
piece

Insert blue fastener

Insert blue fastener

Insert green fastener

Front/Back

Cut 2 each from exterior cotton and interior cotton
Add ¼" (6mm) seam allowance

Cut 2 from lining (no seam allowance)

Cut 2 from
posterboard
¼" (6mm)
smaller than
pattern piece

*Cut out door on
front piece only*

Insert blue fastener

Insert blue fastener

Insert green fastener

Insert green fastener

Dragon Templates: Enlarge all pieces at 400%

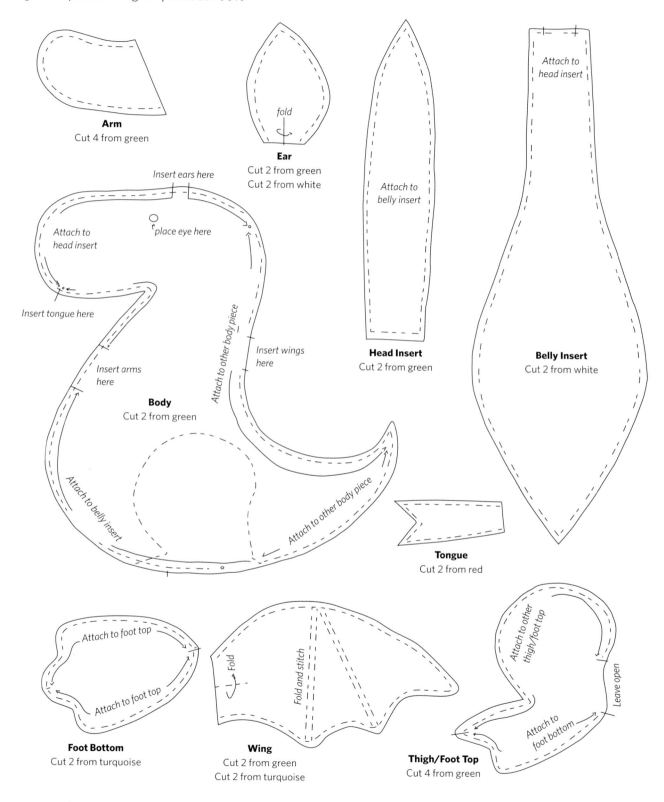

Arm
Cut 4 from green

Ear
Cut 2 from green
Cut 2 from white

fold

Insert ears here

place eye here

Attach to
head insert

Insert tongue here

Insert arms
here

Attach to belly insert

Body
Cut 2 from green

Attach to other body piece

Insert wings
here

Attach to other body piece

Head Insert
Cut 2 from green

Attach to
belly insert

Attach to
head insert

Belly Insert
Cut 2 from white

Tongue
Cut 2 from red

Attach to foot top

Attach to foot top

Foot Bottom
Cut 2 from turquoise

Fold

Fold and stitch

Wing
Cut 2 from green
Cut 2 from turquoise

Attach to other
thigh/foot top

Leave open

Attach to
foot bottom

Thigh/Foot Top
Cut 4 from green

Stone Soup Templates: Enlarge all pieces at 200% except where indicated

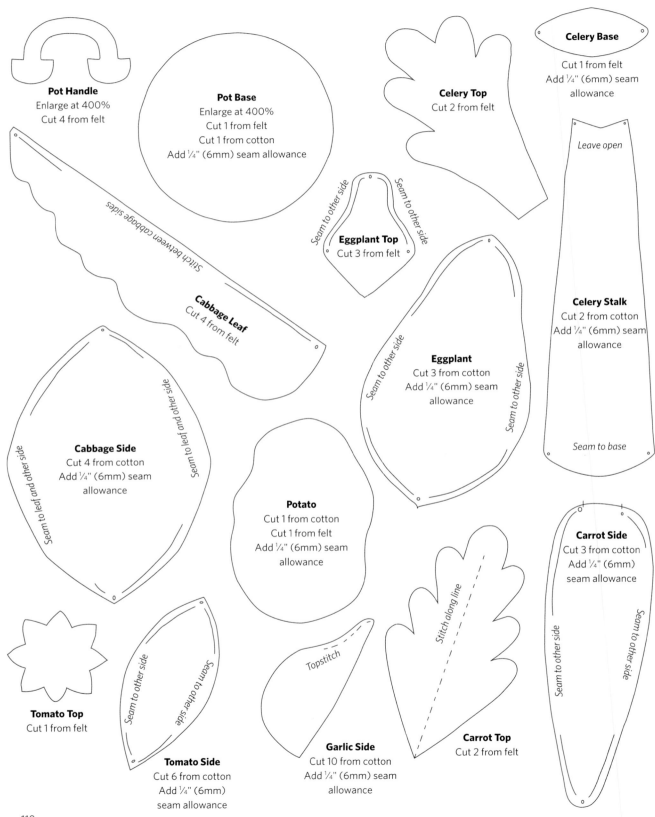

Pot Handle
Enlarge at 400%
Cut 4 from felt

Pot Base
Enlarge at 400%
Cut 1 from felt
Cut 1 from cotton
Add ¼" (6mm) seam allowance

Celery Top
Cut 2 from felt

Celery Base
Cut 1 from felt
Add ¼" (6mm) seam allowance

Leave open

Stitch between cabbage sides

Cabbage Leaf
Cut 4 from felt

Eggplant Top
Cut 3 from felt

Seam to other side

Seam to other side

Celery Stalk
Cut 2 from cotton
Add ¼" (6mm) seam allowance

Seam to base

Seam to leaf and other side

Seam to leaf and other side

Cabbage Side
Cut 4 from cotton
Add ¼" (6mm) seam allowance

Seam to other side

Eggplant
Cut 3 from cotton
Add ¼" (6mm) seam allowance

Seam to other side

Potato
Cut 1 from cotton
Cut 1 from felt
Add ¼" (6mm) seam allowance

Carrot Side
Cut 3 from cotton
Add ¼" (6mm) seam allowance

Stitch along line

Seam to other side

Seam to other side

Tomato Top
Cut 1 from felt

Seam to other side

Seam to other side

Topstitch

Tomato Side
Cut 6 from cotton
Add ¼" (6mm) seam allowance

Garlic Side
Cut 10 from cotton
Add ¼" (6mm) seam allowance

Carrot Top
Cut 2 from felt

Rapunzel and Jack and the Beanstalk Pillow Templates: Enlarge all pieces at 200%

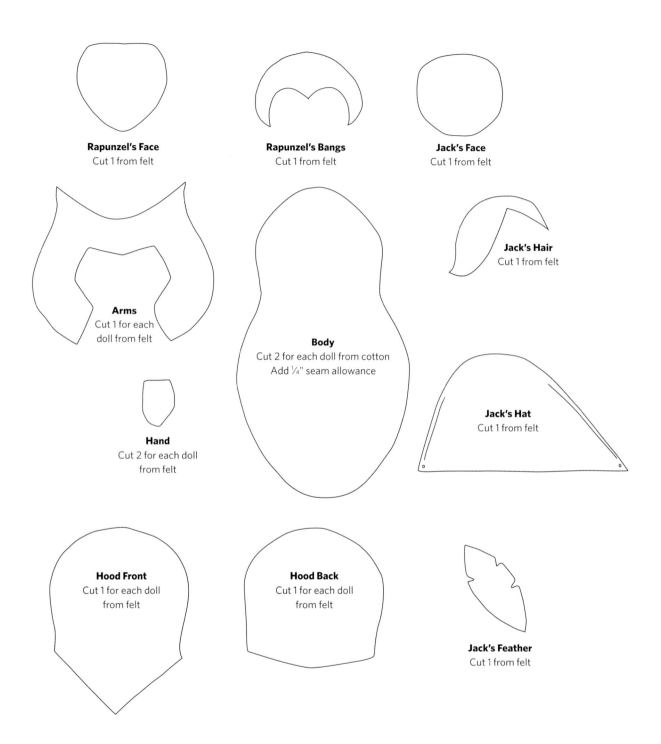

Rapunzel's Face
Cut 1 from felt

Rapunzel's Bangs
Cut 1 from felt

Jack's Face
Cut 1 from felt

Jack's Hair
Cut 1 from felt

Arms
Cut 1 for each
doll from felt

Body
Cut 2 for each doll from cotton
Add ¼" seam allowance

Jack's Hat
Cut 1 from felt

Hand
Cut 2 for each doll
from felt

Hood Front
Cut 1 for each doll
from felt

Hood Back
Cut 1 for each doll
from felt

Jack's Feather
Cut 1 from felt

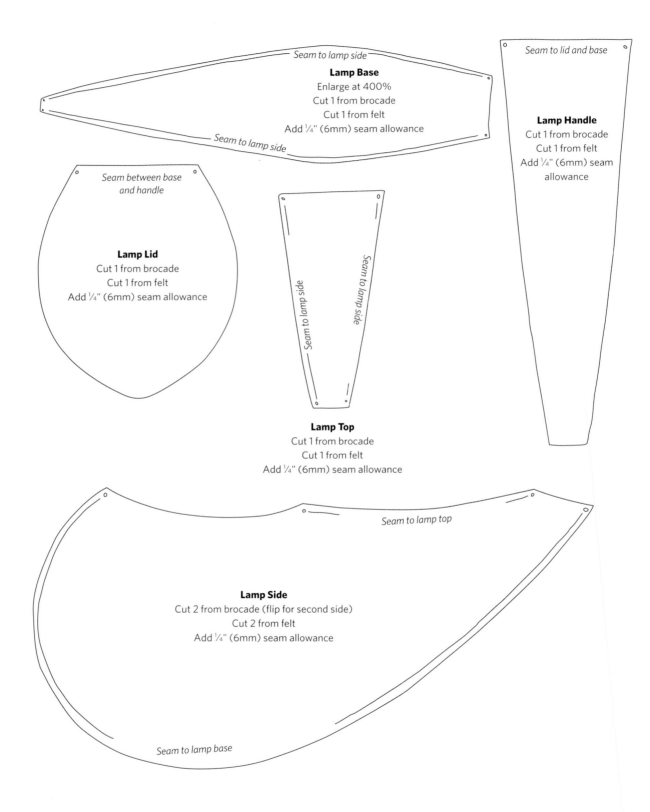

Seam to lamp side

Lamp Base
Enlarge at 400%
Cut 1 from brocade
Cut 1 from felt
Add ¼" (6mm) seam allowance

Seam to lamp side

Seam to lid and base

Lamp Handle
Cut 1 from brocade
Cut 1 from felt
Add ¼" (6mm) seam allowance

Seam between base
and handle

Lamp Lid
Cut 1 from brocade
Cut 1 from felt
Add ¼" (6mm) seam allowance

Seam to lamp side

Seam to lamp side

Lamp Top
Cut 1 from brocade
Cut 1 from felt
Add ¼" (6mm) seam allowance

Seam to lamp top

Lamp Side
Cut 2 from brocade (flip for second side)
Cut 2 from felt
Add ¼" (6mm) seam allowance

Seam to lamp base

Aladdin's Lamp Templates: Enlarge all pieces at 200% except where indicated

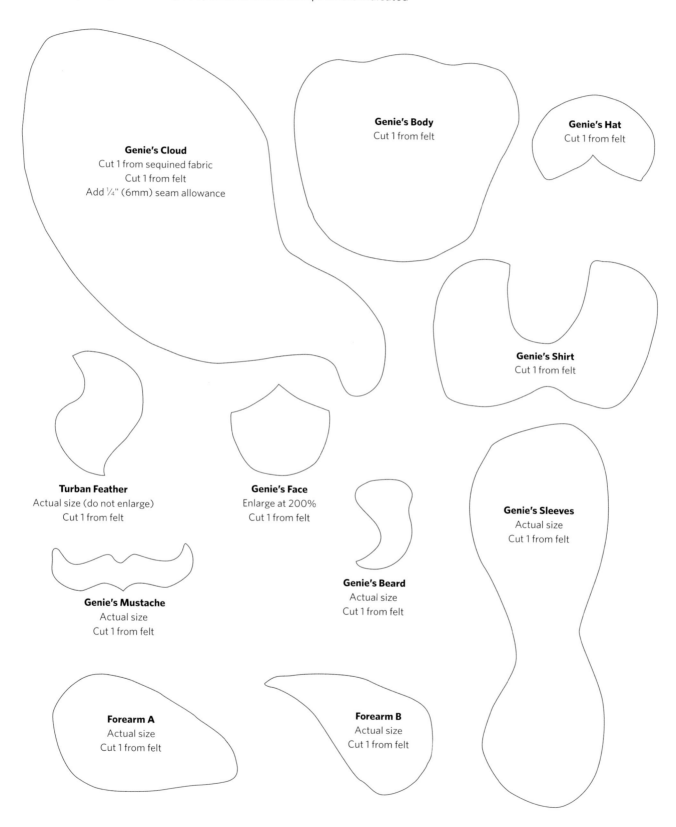

Genie's Cloud
Cut 1 from sequined fabric
Cut 1 from felt
Add ¼" (6mm) seam allowance

Genie's Body
Cut 1 from felt

Genie's Hat
Cut 1 from felt

Genie's Shirt
Cut 1 from felt

Turban Feather
Actual size (do not enlarge)
Cut 1 from felt

Genie's Face
Enlarge at 200%
Cut 1 from felt

Genie's Beard
Actual size
Cut 1 from felt

Genie's Sleeves
Actual size
Cut 1 from felt

Genie's Mustache
Actual size
Cut 1 from felt

Forearm A
Actual size
Cut 1 from felt

Forearm B
Actual size
Cut 1 from felt

Roof Side
Cut 2 each from interior and exterior fabric
Add ¼" (6mm) seam allowance

Roof Front/Back
Cut 2 each from interior and exterior fabric
Add ¼" (6mm) seam allowance

Side Wall
Cut 2 each from interior and exterior fabric
Add ¼" (6mm) seam allowance

Wall Front/Back
Cut 2 each from interior and exterior fabric
Add ¼" (6mm) seam allowance

Wolf Chest
Cut 1 from felt

Wolf Body
Cut 2 from felt

Wolf Nose
Cut 1 from felt

Wolf Face
Cut 1 from felt

Wolf Bandana
Cut 1 from felt

Wolf Tail
Cut 1 from felt

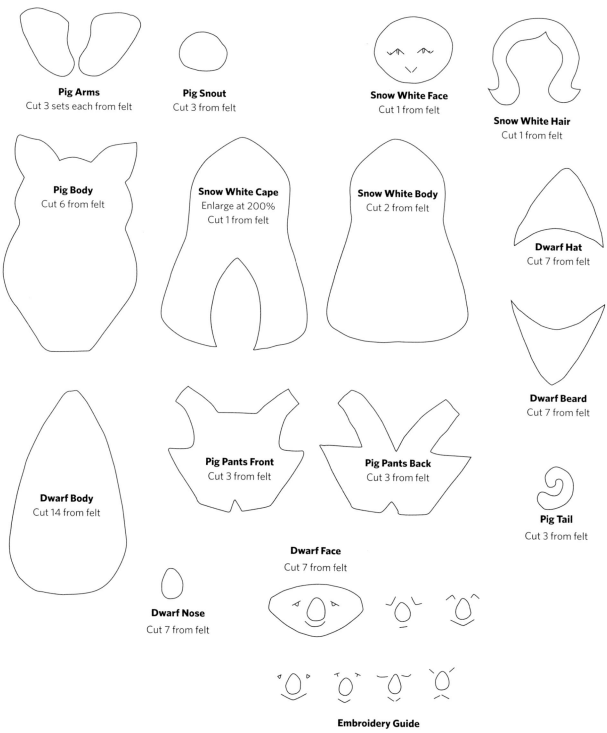

Pig Arms
Cut 3 sets each from felt

Pig Snout
Cut 3 from felt

Snow White Face
Cut 1 from felt

Snow White Hair
Cut 1 from felt

Pig Body
Cut 6 from felt

Snow White Cape
Enlarge at 200%
Cut 1 from felt

Snow White Body
Cut 2 from felt

Dwarf Hat
Cut 7 from felt

Dwarf Beard
Cut 7 from felt

Dwarf Body
Cut 14 from felt

Pig Pants Front
Cut 3 from felt

Pig Pants Back
Cut 3 from felt

Pig Tail
Cut 3 from felt

Dwarf Nose
Cut 7 from felt

Dwarf Face
Cut 7 from felt

Embroidery Guide
Use the embroidery guide to create 7 different expressions

Thumbelina: Enlarge all pieces at 200%

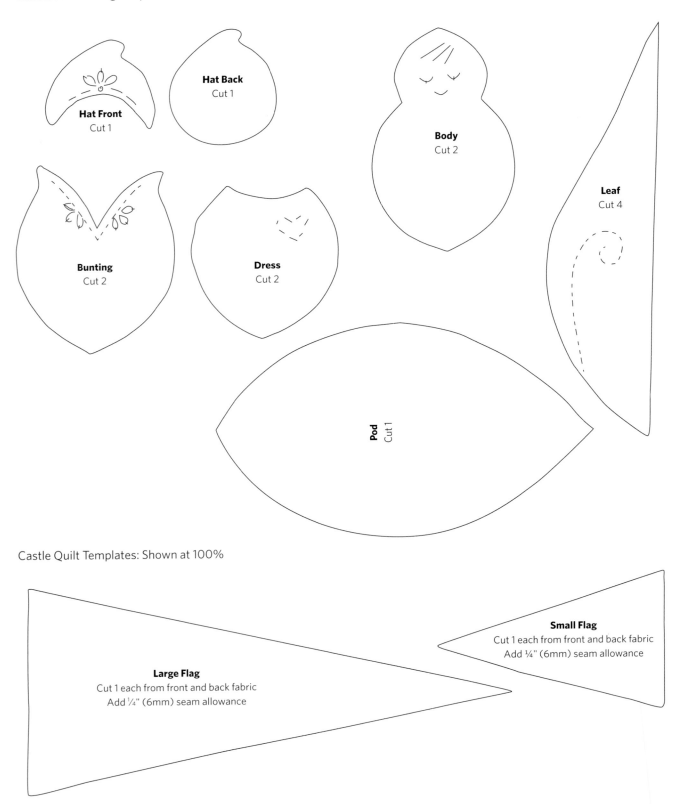

Hat Front
Cut 1

Hat Back
Cut 1

Body
Cut 2

Leaf
Cut 4

Bunting
Cut 2

Dress
Cut 2

Pod
Cut 1

Castle Quilt Templates: Shown at 100%

Large Flag
Cut 1 each from front and back fabric
Add ¼" (6mm) seam allowance

Small Flag
Cut 1 each from front and back fabric
Add ¼" (6mm) seam allowance

Princess and the Pea Templates: Enlarge all pieces at 200%

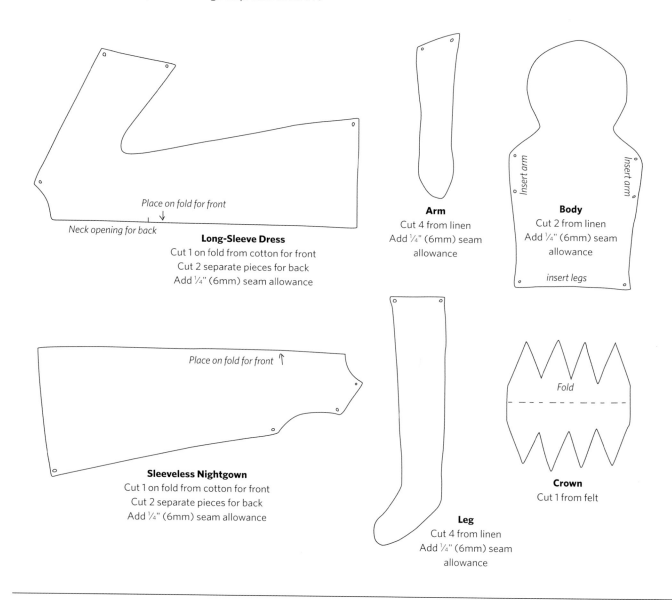

Place on fold for front
↓
Neck opening for back

Long-Sleeve Dress
Cut 1 on fold from cotton for front
Cut 2 separate pieces for back
Add ¼" (6mm) seam allowance

Arm
Cut 4 from linen
Add ¼" (6mm) seam
allowance

Insert arm *Insert arm*

Body
Cut 2 from linen
Add ¼" (6mm) seam
allowance

insert legs

Place on fold for front ↑

Sleeveless Nightgown
Cut 1 on fold from cotton for front
Cut 2 separate pieces for back
Add ¼" (6mm) seam allowance

Fold

Crown
Cut 1 from felt

Leg
Cut 4 from linen
Add ¼" (6mm) seam
allowance

METRIC CONVERSION CHART

To convert	to	multiply by
Inches	Centimeters	2.54
Centimeters	Inches	0.4
Feet	Centimeters	30.5
Centimeters	Feet	0.03
Yards	Meters	0.9
Meters	Yards	1.1

Index

www.fwmedia.com

18 17 16 15 14   5 4 3 2 1

Distributed in Canada by Fraser Direct
100 Armstrong Avenue
Georgetown, ON, Canada L7G 5S4
Tel: (905) 877-4411

Distributed in the U.K. and Europe by F+W MEDIA INTERNATIONAL
Brunel House, Newton Abbot, Devon, TQ12 4PU, England
Tel: (+44) 1626 323200, Fax: (+44) 1626 323319
Email: postmaster@davidandcharles.co.uk

Distributed in Australia by Capricorn Link
P.O. Box 704, S. Windsor NSW, 2756 Australia
Tel: (02) 4560 1600, Fax: (02) 4577 5288
E-mail: books@capricornlink.com.au

SRN: U9384
ISBN-13: 978-1-4402-3962-5

Edited by Stephanie White
Designed by Clare Finney; cover by Kelly Pace
Production coordinated by Greg Nock
Photography by Christine Polomsky
Illustrations by Heidi Boyd

Appearing in this book are excerpts quoted from:

Unicorns! Unicorns! by Geraldine McCaughrean and illustrated by Sophie Windham. London: Orchard Books, 1997.

Saint George and the Dragon by Margaret Hodges and illustrated by Irina Schart Hyman. New York: Little, Brown, 1984.

Dedication

Dedicated to my Sweet Celia; thank you for sharing so many wonderful books with me, for being my ever present tester and expert design consultant.

Acknowledgements

Huge thanks to National Nonwovens, Cloud 9 fabrics, Monuluna, Riley and Blake who graciously provided material for the designs in this book.

I received wonderful technical advice and trouble shooting from my local sewing store. If you're ever stuck, find your way to the cutting table and ask your local experts. I credit them with the clever exposed hook and loop fastener in the play totes, and the liner that prevents the brocade from fraying in Aladdin's lamp.

Hugs to my good friend and creative neighbor Deb, who walked me through assembling my very first quilt.

I have the most supportive family who graciously puts up with the detritus of my creative career; they tolerate fabric scraps in the dining room and expertly navigate a project strewn couch. I love you to Neverland and beyond.

About the Author

Heidi Boyd is the author of fifteen craft books, ranging from recycled crafting to beading and sewing. She is the creator of Whimsy Kits & Stitches, a line of felt stitching kits.

When she's not working on kits, workshops and publishing projects, Heidi, her husband Jon, their three children and their dog Otto actively enjoy the natural beauty of their midcoast Maine home.

Find Heidi Boyd at her website www.heidiboyd.com
Follow her on Twitter: @heidiboydcrafts
Like her on Facebook: www.facebook.com/HeidiBoydWhimsyKits

Whimsy Kits are available at www.etsy.com/shop/heidiboydwhimsykits

More inspiration awaits!

Find these and other fine Fons & Porter publications at your favorite retailer.

Stitched Whimsy
Heidi Boyd

Make 20 adorable sewn, stitched and felted projects, complete with clear instructions, helpful illustrations and crisp patterns. Whether you're new to sewing or a long-time stitcher, you'll find something to love in this book. Grab your needles, threads, fabrics and felt and sew along with Stitched Whimsy!

Sewing Tales to Stitch and Love
Kerry Goulder

Bring 18 charming characters and their stories to life through the magic of needle and thread! Inside *Sewing Tales to Stitch and Love* is an irresistible collection of sewn and stuffed toys that all ages will love. Delightful and durable, these once-upon-a-time creations are made to be played with endlessly and cherished forever after!

Stitch Magazine
Creating With Fabric + Thread

Stitch is the favorite magazine of modern sewists everywhere, featuring vintage modern patterns, embellishment techniques, and modern embroidery designs to name a few. A full size pattern pullout is included in every issue. Whether you love bags, clothing, pillows, or other home decor, you are going to love creating the beautiful handmade items you find in *Stitch*. We know you will love every issue.

Join Sew Daily and you can interact with thousands of other sewing enthusiasts! Whether you sew clothing, accessories, home decor items, or just love the possibilities of fabric and thread, you'll find all sorts of great information....and make new friends, too! Visit www.sewdaily.com